Protestation

In all that I shall say in this book I submit to what is taught by Our mother, the Holy Roman Church; if there is anything in it contrary to this, it will be without my knowledge. Therefore, for the love of Our Lord, I beg the learned men who are to read it to look at it very carefully and to make known to me any faults of this nature which there may be in it and the many others that it will have of other kinds. If there is anything good in it, let this be to the greater glory and honor of God in the service of His most sacred Mother, our Patroness and Lady, to whom I am, though all unworthy, bound and consecrated as a slave.

Timothy Flanders

This book is dedicated to my children.

Sanctae Dei Genetrici
In signum
Gratitudinis et filialis obedientiae.

In thanksgiving to God for ten years as a Catholic

In thanksgiving for eleven years
a consecrated slave of the Immaculata

AMGD

WHEN THE GATES OF HELL PREVAIL

WHAT CATHOLICS DO IN DARK TIMES

Timothy S. Flanders

WHEN THE GATES OF HELL PREVAIL

What Catholics Do in Dark Times

TIMOTHY S. FLANDERS

© Our Lady of Victory Press, MMXXIII

ISBN 979-8-9877607-4-1

Our Lady of Victory Press is an imprint of The Meaning of Catholic, a lay apostolate dedicated to uniting Catholics against the enemies of Holy Church.
MeaningofCatholic.com

Design and layout by W. Flanders.

Our Lady of Victory, pray for us!

Table of Contents

Part I
When the Darkness Can Be Felt

Part II
The First and Greatest Commandment

Part III
The Second Greatest Commandment

Part IV
Jesus is King!

Preface

Please be assured, dear reader, that no virtues described in this book, nor ideals discussed or wisdom propounded, is the possession or achievement of the author. It is rather the inheritance of all of us from our holy fathers, of which I will attempt to speak in these pages. These considerations are things that have helped me in this time, and perhaps they will help you, also.

I hope that, by your prayers, we may be made worthy to join the company of our fathers and mothers who came before us in suffering in our time for the one Faith delivered to the saints. And that it may be our joy and our peace to share this with our children.

The first part of this text attempts to start from the point when the *darkness can be felt* (Ex. x. 21). This point is something that every soul must pass through in order to advance in the spiritual life. It is poignantly described by the Prophet in Psalm LXXXVIII when at first the Holy Spirit exults to say *Neither will I profane my covenant: and the words that proceed from my mouth I will not make void*, and yet a few verses later laments: *Thou hast overthrown the covenant of thy servant: thou hast profaned his sanctuary on the earth*. It is this apparent contradiction that brings about the darkness which can be felt. This is the reason for the title of this book, which tries to describe this apparent contradiction, which seems to prove God false, yet is later revealed to be a deeper mystery. This is the subject of the first part of this book.

The next parts deal then with the primary and secondary priorities of all of our forefathers in such times, with practical recommendations to follow those aims. The final part treats on spiritual and liturgical applications that help to bring to fruition the spiritual priorities already explained.

This text will not deal with the question of the Papacy very much, as this is reserved for another forthcoming book by the author. Rather, this text is concerned about the thing that all our forefathers focused on in dark times—and it's not the Pope. I hope that by mostly ignoring this topic this book will help re-orient the reader toward a more traditional, pre-modern stance toward the Vatican.

Without any doubt, with absolute certainty, we can say this: our children, or our children's children, or some future generation of the Church militant will see it—the liberty and exaltation of Holy Mother Church.

In the meantime let us fix the eyes of our hearts on the Church triumphant and suffering, and fight the good fight as our fathers have done: to be made worthy to suffer for the Name of Jesus. Otherwise, we are unworthy of the name "Christian."

In the words of the Greek liturgy, "Through the prayers of our holy fathers, Lord Jesus Christ our God, have mercy on us and save us, amen."

T. S. F.
The Immaculate Conception
In the year 2023
of the reign of Our Lord Jesus Christ the King

PART I
WHEN THE DARKNESS CAN BE FELT

I

Every 250 Years
the Church Faces Certain Destruction

In my study of history, I've noticed a few patterns. One of these is the cycle of impossible situations. It seems that about every ten generations—two hundred and fifty years, sometimes less—the Church is faced with one of these. It is some crisis which threatens to the destroy the whole Church and prove God false. At the time, it is unprecedented—unlike anything the Church has faced up to that point. During such a crisis many think that the world is at an end and start to identify the Antichrist among their contemporaries. Apocalyptic literature begins to proliferate. Yet somehow, against all odds, God delivers His Church once again.

The Lord's military strategy for Gideon was to reduce his army from 32,000 to 300 *lest Israel should glory against me, and say: I was delivered by my own strength* (Jdg. vii. 2). This tactic doesn't seem to have changed over the years. If Church history shows us anything, it is that the "liberty and exaltation of Holy Mother Church" *with men is impossible: but with God all things are possible* (Mt. xix. 26). I think it is important for us to remember these things in order to face our own situation. So here I will review a few of these in succession.[1]

Crucifixion and Persecution (33-313)

The Church was born out of the most devasting crisis—the crucifixion of Christ. Against every conception of human

---

[1] For a more detailed survey of these impossible situations, see T. S. Flanders, *City of God vs. City of Man* (Our Lady of Victory Press, 2021).

imaginings, Our Lord arose and sent them power from on high. Emboldened, they faced the persecution of the Jews and the Romans (the latter being the fiercest empire the world had ever known). St. Paul traveled throughout the empire boldly proclaiming Christ the King.

But even at the death of the last Apostle, the Church was a tiny movement with a handful of adherents which almost no one believed would amount to anything. The triumph predicted in the book of Revelation must have seemed like raving lunacy in 100 AD. The Church was mercilessly and systematically persecuted again and again by the Roman Empire, and somehow they endured and conquered. In 301, Armenia converted. In 313, Constantine revoked the persecutions and began favoring the Church. Suddenly the unthinkable began to happen.

The Arian Crisis (321-381)

No sooner was a shocking triumph begun for the Church but a new crisis arose which quickly engulfed the faithful. The vast majority of bishops denied the divinity of Christ. The stalwart defender of orthodoxy seemed to be only a single bishop, who was mocked as a lunatic with the phrase *Athanasius contra mundum* ("Athanasius against the world"). It was a brave new Arian world as Jerome lamented, "The whole world groaned, and was astonished to find itself Arian."

The emperors renewed the persecution against the orthodox, and paganism was even revived by Julian the Apostate. Athanasius was driven from his see again and again. Martyrs shed their blood once more. Churches were seized for the Arian creed. All bishops seemed to abandon the faith as well as Pope Liberius. The laity were left alone to fight for truth. Yet once again, against all odds, this raging heresy was beaten back.

The Sassanian and Muhammadan Invasions (602-661)

But as the generations of Arians died away (in the east), a new fracture appeared in Christendom: Monophysitism. This heresy became the cause of the first lasting schism between East and west (the Acadian schism 484-519). It continued as the bishops attempted to resolve it over the successive generations, but by the 6th century bloodshed began to increase between the factions of Christians. While the west was grappling with barbarism, the stability of the east was breaking down as well.

The crisis took a turn for the worse when the divided Eastern Roman Empire could not withstand the incursions of the Sassanians beginning in 602. They penetrated to the Holy City of Jerusalem and even captured the True Cross. The situation was dire, provoking Emperor Heraclius to lead a crusade and recover the True Cross. But he too fell into heresy with another compromise with truth called Monothelitism.

Then the most devastating force arose on the frontier: an army of Arabs with a neo-Arian creed who quickly conquered most of the Christian lands in the East. At this point men were sure that the Apocalypse had come upon them, and numerous eschatological theories were put forth. But a new Athanasius arose who defeated Monothelitism: Maximus the Confessor against the world. The heresy was condemned and the advance of Muhammad was checked.

The First Pornocracy and the Viking Invasion (882-964)

Later, even as the east was experiencing its last great heresy under Iconoclasm, the west experienced a revival and advance under Charlemagne. But around this time a new menace emerged: the Northmen ("Vikings") who devastated western Europe like no one had seen before. A new petition was added to various oral litanies: *from the fury of the Northmen, deliver us O Lord.* They raped and pillaged across the continent, singling out monasteries for destruction.

To make matters worse, the Roman see fell into its first sustained period of corruption. It was a period later known as the Pornocracy, due to the unspeakable acts of sacrilege, profanation, and debauchery committed by the popes and their allies in this time. This hit rock bottom with John XII, the most corrupt pope of all.

The people of Rome rebelled against him and the pious Emperor Otto I helped depose the pope and turn the tide against evil men in the hierarchy. This led eventually to the Cluniac reform to cleanse the clergy. Within a few generations St. Peter Damien (1007-1073) was leading the charge against clerical abuse, and shortly later the Gospel was conquering the vicious Northmen. The barbarity of our fathers was being turned into the chivalry of knights for Christendom.

The Great Western Schism (1378-1417)

After a great period of revival in the Church with the glorious 13th century and the Crusade in Southern France and the continued success in Spain, the Church again fell into a period of decline. First, the papacy became the pawn of French politics, a period known as the Avignon Papacy (1309-1376), named for its residence in modern France. This papal palace saw seven popes and five antipopes. Within a generation of this unhappy circumstance, France and England abandoned the glory of the crusade in favor of fighting each other in the Hundred Years War (1337-1453). Then the Black Death hit Europe, which peaked in 1348, and struck dead about half of the population. Bodies were stacked in the streets.

If this situation weren't bad enough, the Great Western schism broke out in which Europe divided between two different popes. And then a third pope was added. Ecclesiastical revolt was gaining steam between Ockham (d. 1347), Wycliffe (d. 1384), and Huss (d. 1415). Despite this darkness, figure sius arose, the miracle-working preacher St. Vincent Ferrer (1350-1419). He is credited with turning back the apocalypse that everyone thought was coming down upon the world. He convinced the adherents of antipope Benedict XIII (whom he himself believed to be the true pope) to remove their obedience from him and give it to the Council of Constance, which eventually resolved the schism.

The Second Pornocracy and the Protestant Looters' Revolt (1517-1563)

But once again the Church fell into decline as the Renaissance popes took control. The Black Death seems to have killed off most of the good priests, and by 1500 there was widespread debauchery and corruption, while the papacy followed suit with the worst of the worldly. We may call this time the Second Pornocracy due to its imitation of the First. Luther went to Rome and the scandal helped provoke him.

Suddenly Europe erupted in civil war as Protestants began revolting, looting churches and destroying statues. It was the Second Iconoclasm. Princes and kings joined the movement so they could commit adultery and theft with impunity, and were not above getting military aid from the Muhammadans to fight Catholics. The papacy was mired in corruption, and hesitated desperately to address the situation for almost thirty years while destruction reigned.

Finally, with the great efforts of new saints, the Council of Trent was convened and decreed its anathemas. Despite fierce opposition even from Catholic kings, the Council succinctly clarified the vast majority of Catholic doctrine under attack and laid out the basic program of true reform. Within a few generations the Catholic Church was back on the offensive, winning back souls to the Church and stopping the advance of Protestantism in Europe. More than this, they began to spread the faith throughout the world from China to Japan to North and South America.

The Liberal Revolutions (1789-1800)[2]

But even as the Counter-Reformation gained momentum, Pope Urban VIII betrayed the faith. He induced France to side with the Protestants in the Thirty Years War (1618-1648), which turned the tide in favor of the heretics. As France became increasingly secular in the 1700s, a wave of anti-Catholic sentiment stirred among the elites who sought a way out of Catholic order. Finally in 1789, inspired by the American revolutionaries, the French began the revolt known as the French Revolution. This targeted the Church for genocidal attacks and mass murder, helped to justify pornography as free speech, and started to replace Catholic tradition with Liberal public education.

Eventually this movement turned into an empire, and Napoleon conquested most of Europe, destroying the Catholic infrastructure everywhere. He captured the pope and brought him to France where he died. The enemies of the faith were proclaiming their victory over the old Catholic order by 1800.

But once again a revival took place, against all opposition. The papacy was revived and the Romantic and Ultramontane movements set off a renewal of Catholicism across Europe. France finally began implementing the Council of Trent, and even restoring Gregorian Chant (which had fallen into widespread disuse even in Rome). Bl. Pius IX and Leo XIII both worked to bring about a counter-revolution of Catholicism, and especially Thomism after 1879.

The Third Pornocracy and the New Iconoclasm (1965-Present)

But the world responded by killing each other on the most massive scale ever seen in two world wars, refusing to repent even after the Miracle of the Sun. The errors of Russia spread and eventually found their way into the Church. Corrupt men

[2] The term "Liberal" in this book refers to the socio-political heresy of Liberalism condemned by the Magisterium of the 19th century.

began wielding power in the Vatican, and by 1965 a violent New Iconoclasm had arisen. The popes and bishops responded with timidity, allowing widespread destruction of statues, churches, liturgy and theology. Marriage began to break down across the world, and the unborn holocaust spread its silent bloodshed. In the late 1970s, the dossier of Cardinal Gagnon showed Paul VI that he was living in the Third Pornocracy, in which the debauchery gripping the Vatican had once against reached nadir levels. John Paul II hesitated to crack down on it, and by the time Benedict began to act, the evil machine was too strong for him to control. And then Pope Francis.

This story is known all too well. But when we look at the context of history, I think it is easier to see our present darkness, though unprecedented, as something that God can handle. And He will. Let us consider the faith of our fathers and the saints who continued the tradition of Athanasius against the world. God permits these things so that we may not ascribe to ourselves any sort of glory, since no man can fix the new unprecedented crisis we face. It is literally impossible to resolve. But not for Almighty God. Let us pass down the faith to our children and never lose hope.

II

When the Gates of Hell Prevail
Over the Church

"The Gates of Hell Will Not Prevail."

Many Catholics today utter this phrase to justify their opinions about the crisis of today's Holy Church. Some "Conservatives" say that since the gates of Hell cannot prevail against the Church, an infiltration cannot possibly have happened. Sedevacantists say that since an infiltration has happened, and the gates of Hell cannot prevail, then the official Church must be a façade and the true Church is their underground sect. Still other Catholics, finally exhausted with the cognitive dissonance necessary to justify strange behavior from the pope, become convinced that the gates of Hell *have* prevailed over the Papacy. They are then taken in by lies from the Greek schismatics and give themselves over to the imaginary unity of the Greek schism.

But in each of these cases it seems the interpretation of the phrase "will not prevail," ultimately relics *on a private judgment*. As we shall see, the Church has only ascribed general meanings to this promise, not specific circumstances.

In the times past already discussed, our fathers have thought circumstances were so dire in their day that the end of the world was imminent. It is hard for us to imagine the feeling of facing the type of widespread bloodshed that our fathers' faced. Some lost hope, others persevered.

If we say that in those times the gates of Hell did *not* prevail, at what point would we say that they have prevailed? How bad does it really have to get? How can we trust in a promise whose object is unclear? Let us consider the

Sacred Scripture and the Holy Fathers and, with God's help, attempt to answer these questions.

Holy Scripture

Our Lord has just multiplied loaves and miraculously fed four thousand on a mountain near the sea of Galilee. He comes to a nearby coastal town and is confronted by the Pharisees and Sadducees. They demand from him a sign from heaven. The Lord rebukes them and promises no sign but the sign of Jonas. He then sails with his disciples and warns them against the doctrine of the Pharisees and Sadducees. They disembark and walk north together many miles.

They reach the northern border town of Caesarea Philippi, near the ancient territory of the lost idolatrous tribe of Dan, where the pagans have dedicated the surrounding rocks and grottos to their many gods. It is here that Our Lord demands and receives the confession of the Incarnation from St. Peter: *"Thou art Christ, the Son of the living God."* Our Lord responds by calling him the Blessed Son of Jonas, the One Who Listens (*"Simon"*) to the revelation from "My Father in Heaven." He then speaks of his person and his confession and utters these words over him:

> I say to thee: That thou art Peter; and upon this rock I will build my church, and the gates of hell shall not prevail against it.

> Ego dico tibi, quia tu es Petrus, et super hanc petram ædificabo Ecclesiam meam, et portæ inferi non prævalebunt adversus eam.

> κἀγὼ δέ σοι λέγω ὅτι σὺ εἶ Πέτρος, καὶ ἐπὶ ταύτῃ τῇ πέτρᾳ οἰκοδομήσω μου τὴν ἐκκλησίαν, καὶ πύλαι ᾅδου οὐ κατισχύσουσιν αὐτῆς.

23

Here in the context of Caesarea Phillipi, we may observe a few things about these words. First, the immediate context is the grotto at Caesarea Phillipi, where the rocky crags held the idols of many gods. The men who were killed and sacrificed to these demon gods were thrown into a pit in the rock known as the "gates of Hell."[3] In addition, the city itself was the site of large construction projects by the late king Herod Philip and the current king, Herod Agrippa II. All of these things would be immediately apparent.

The words also bring to mind the foundation rock of the Second Temple at Jersusalem (*eben shetiyyah*) which sealed off a long shaft in the earth leading to *sheol* (Hades). His words about building also recall the great kings of Israel, David and Solomon (in contrast to the false builder king Herod). David laid the preparations and Solomon did the construction of the First Temple.

Thus in the context of many rocks, gates of Hell and construction, Our Lord tells of His own chosen rock and building. The gates (πύλαι) refer to the defensive structure seen at the entrance to any city, thus invoking the expansion of the City of God against the defenses of the City of Man of the Evil one. The verb overcome (κατισχύσουσιν) thus implies the failure of a siege to penetrate the gates of a city.

Moreover, Our Lord calls Simon the "Rock" (Πέτρος, *Petros*), which in Greek had a connotation of a weapon, such as was used in Homer and by King David to slay Goliath, thus connecting with the defensive imagery of the gates. And given the above context he refers to St. Peter's confession as a "rock"

---

[3] In both Old Testament and Greek thought, "Hades" (Sheol, "the grave," "the netherworld,") was a place where all souls went after death, whether good or bad. It was a place under the earth for these souls to stay indefinitely. Both Greek (Odysseus) and Roman (Aeneaus) heroes traveled to Hades and conversed with the souls there. "Hell" as the grave (*Sheol*) or "Hades" is different than the Hell of eternal punishment (*Gehenna*). Unfortunately these two different places get translated into English with the same word "Hell." Nevertheless Hell as "Hades" and Hell as Gehenna bare a certain resemblance in their lack of hope, and sometimes they are used interchangeably in a more general sense.

(πέτρᾳ) which was the feminine form of the Greek "stone," making its meaning refer to the rock foundation of a building. By using the same word in two forms, he also integrates the foundational person with the foundational confession. The person and his confession become a *weapon* against which the defensive structure of hell will not prevail.

Finally, the word used for build (οἰκοδομήσω μου τὴν ἐκκλησίαν) holds the meaning of constructing a building from a foundation, utilizing the same words used in reference to Solomon (I Para. xxii. 10). But the word also has the prefix οἰκο- which refers to the forming of a household. Thus the whole phrase brings together the persons (both the foundational person named Rock and the Church), the confession (foundation rock) and the institution to be built, all in opposition to the rival power of Hell whose defenses will not be able to withstand the expansion of the Church.

Immediately following this, Our Lord tells of His coming death and resurrection, prompting the aforementioned Rock to rebuke Jesus Himself. Our Lord then calls St. Peter a different name: "Get behind me, Satan." Herein is a mystery tied closely to our text on the gates of Hell. When Simon hears and confesses the foundation rock (the Incarnation), he is his own name: the Rock against the gates of Hell. When he denies the corollary of the Incarnation (the Cross of suffering), he becomes Satan. Yet his name was changed to Rock, not Satan. And although he can become Satan, his name and his person do not change. This is a great mystery to which we will return below.

When the Gates of Hell Prevailed

Among the many meanings of the gates of Hell, the most obvious and immediate is simply natural death. Thus the name for the pit of corpses at Caesarea Philippi. Jews and Greeks both believed that after a man died his soul passed through the gates of Hell (or "Hades") and was left there indefinitely. There was no hope of getting out of this place.

When Our Lord was crucified, the gates of Hell *did* prevail over the Church, the Body of Christ.

Jesus Christ was dead.

His soul went to Hell and his body was laid in the tomb.[4]

Let us pause for a moment and consider the reality that the disciples faced here. They had left their families. They had left their homes and livelihoods to follow Jesus Christ because they believed and hoped in Him.

And now He was dead.

We hoped that it was he that should have redeemed Israel (Lk. xxiv. 21). Their hope was completely lost, and now they feared for their own lives also. What dark despair was theirs at this moment! Everything visible showed clearly that the gates of Hell had prevailed. No man could deny it.

The only person who would deny this would be Our Lady, who might have seemed to the disciples to be drawn away into a mother's excess. But it is the disciples that the Lord would rebuke: *O foolish and slow of heart to believe in all things, Which the prophets have spoken* (Lk. xxiv. 25).

Our Lady kept faith on Holy Saturday, and we celebrate her on Saturdays ever since (more on that in the next chapter). For the triumph of Hell was only for those seeing with the eyes of the flesh, not with the eyes of faith. On the contrary, Our Lord descended into hell in order to destroy its gates. As it is said:

> In the grave with the body
> But in Hades with the soul
> In Paradise with the thief
> And on the throne with the Father and the Spirit
> Wast Thou, O Christ, filling all things
> Thyself uncircumscribed.[5]

---

[4] Thus the Apostles creed says *descendit ad inferos* ("descended into hell"). The definition of "dead" is the moment when the soul separates from the body.

[5] Liturgy of St. John Chrysostom.

26

It is here that we know what is meant in the creed, "He descended into hell," and in the phrase from St. Peter: *In which also coming he preached to those spirits that were in prison: Which had been some time incredulous, when they waited for the patience of God in the days of Noe* (I Pt. iii. 19).

But in the Body of Christ was contained all the Body of the faithful to come—the whole Church militant, triumphant and suffering. In the true death of Jesus Christ, the entire Church was scattered and destroyed and put to death. It may be piously believed that there was not a single Christian remaining upon earth on that day—save only our All-Holy Lady.

Thus when we consider the question of the gates of Hell, we must recall this first initial triumph of the Devil, when our God allowed him to triumph. When our God permitted Himself to be carried captive through the gates of Hell. Can any tragedy in the Church compare to the silence of God on Holy Saturday? *By every reasonable standard by which men can judge anything, the gates of Hell had prevailed.*

But against all expectations, Our Lord kept His promise, and the gates of Hell were overthrown. Thus we see in the Greek Resurrection icon the gates of Hell being torn asunder and Satan bound in chains beneath. Adam and Eve are lifted up out of Hades.

This very real triumph of Hell—at least according to all things natural and visible—must be deeply contemplated by every Christian. We must consider: if while Our Lord walked the earth, the gates of Hell destroyed the Church, the Body of Christ, so utterly and completely, how much more will the Church be overthrown in times to come? And yet how much more miraculous will be the Church's glorious resurrection?

Holy Tradition

Having considered the meaning of the Scripture, let us rely now on the Fathers to give us the proper meaning of this promise. As it is written:

27

Stand in the multitude of ancients that are wise,
and join thyself from thy heart to their wisdom,
that thou mayst hear every discourse of God, and
the sayings of praise may not escape thee. And if
thou see a man of understanding, go to him early
in the morning, and let thy foot wear the steps of
his doors (Ecclus. vi. 35).

It is crucial to seize upon the fact that as Catholics, we are
not free to make our own opinion about the promise. We are
bound to hold to what our fathers held, and not presume
ourselves wise enough to conclude something against their
wisdom. Therefore what was said above we submit to the
judgment of Tradition.

How have the Fathers understood this promise? As with
other passages, there are multiple layers of meaning. Hilary
says it means the triumph over death, while Origen and Jerome
say it is sin and heresy that will not overcome the Church
(*Catena Aurea*). St. John Chrysostom connects the promise to
Our Lord's resurrection (*Hom.* LIV), as does Ambrose
(*Christian Faith*, IV 2.14) but Ambrose adds that the promise
applies also to the person of Peter (2.26). Another patristic
interpretation says that Our Lord is promising that the gates
"shall not separate the Church from the love and faith of Me"
(*Catena Aurea*). Summing up the many interpretations of the
Fathers, Bede says:

The gates of Hades are depraved teachings,
which by seducing the imprudent draw them
down there. The gates of Hades are also the
torments and banishments of persecutors,
which either by frightening or by cajoling any
of the weak away from the stability of the faith,
open to them the entrance into everlasting
death. But also the wrong-headed works of the
unfaithful, or their silly conversations, are

surely the gates of Hades, inasmuch as they show their hearers and followers the path of perdition. Many are the gates of Hades, but none of them prevails over the Church that has been founded upon the Rock (*Hom.* I.20 *Homilies on the Gospels*, Bk I, 201).

St. Thomas also later writes about the many layers of meaning:

What are the gates of Hell? Heretics: for, just as through a door a man goes into a house, through them a man goes into Hell. Likewise tyrants, demons and sins. And however much through heretics other churches can be blamed, nevertheless the Roman Church has not been corrupted by heretics because it was founded upon the rock. Thus the heretics were in Constantinople, and the labor of the Apostles was lost. Only the Church of Peter has remained inviolate. Thus it is said *I have prayed for thee, Peter, that thy faith fail not* (Lk. xxii. 32). And this not only refers to the Church of Peter but to the faith of Peter, and to the whole Western Church. Hence I hold that the Westerners ought to have a greater reverence for Peter than the other Apostles (*Commentary on Matthew*).[6]

---

[6] Translation my own. "*Et qui sunt portae Inferi? Haeretici: quia sicut per portam intratur in domum, sic per istos intratur in Infernum. Item tyranni, Daemones, peccata. Et quamvis aliae Ecclesiae vituperari possint per haereticos, Ecclesia tamen Romana non fuit ab haereticis depravataquia supra petram erat fundata. Unde in Constantinopoli fuerunt haeretici, et labor apostolorum amissus erat; sola Petri Ecclesia inviolata permansit. Unde Lc. XXII, 32: ego rogavi pro te, Petre, ut non deficiat fides tua. Et hoc non solum refertur ad Ecclesiam Petri, sed ad fidem Petri, et ad totam Occidentalem Ecclesiam. Unde credo quod Occidentales maiorem reverentiam debent Petro, quam aliis apostolis.*"

But how can the Roman Church be inviolate if, even by St. Thomas' day, Honorius had been anathematized, Stephen VII's decree on ordinations had been invalidated, John XII had toasted Satan, and Paschal II's erroneous investiture decree had been condemned by St. Bruno as "heresy"? In our own time, who can deny that heretics have corrupted Rome? This is a great mystery. Vatican I dogmatized it by placing stringent conditions on papal infallibility. But this left other questions unanswered. We have treated this in another place, but here let us bring to bear our passage on this question.[7]

Peter, Satan and the Roman Papacy

First, let us briefly review the meaning of the Petrine primacy. Because of second millennium emergencies, the Roman See has been obliged to emphasize her own primacy more and more, and it can be forgotten that this passage refers to every bishop as well. The Fathers see every bishop as holding the Petrine promise as long as they are united to the body of Church.[8] The determining factor for this is

---

[7] See T. S. Flanders, "On the Limits of Papal Infallibility," *OnePeterFive* (June 29, 2022). <https://onepeterfive.com/limits-papal-infallibility/>.

[8] "A very clear patristic tradition sees the succession of Peter in the episcopal ministry. The doctrine of St Cyprian of Carthage on the 'See of Peter' being present in every local Church, and not only in Rome, is well-known. It is also found in the East, among people who certainly never read the *De unitate ecclesia* of Cyprian, but who share its main idea, thus witnessing to it as part of the catholic tradition of the Church. St Gregory of Nyssa, for example, affirms that Christ 'through Peter gave to the bishops the keys of the heavenly honors,' and the author of the *Areopagitica*, when speaking of the 'hierarchs' of the Church, refers immediately to the image of St Peter. A careful analysis of ecclesiastical literature both Eastern and Western, of the first millennium, including such documents as the lives of the saint, would certainly show that this tradition was a persistent one; and indeed it belongs to the essence of Christian ecclesiology to consider any local bishop to be the teacher of his flock and therefore to fulfill sacramentally, through apostolic

communion with the Roman See. Other Sees were founded by St. Peter but here alone did the Prince of the Apostles receive his crown of martyrdom. Thus very early (2nd century) the evidence is clear that the prerogatives of the Roman See included governing the entire Church.[9]

Sometimes non-Catholics will emphasize other aspects of this passage to attempt to exclude the Roman aspect, such as saying the promise refers to his confession, not his person, or such things. It is true that the Fathers appear to make a distinction between the confession and the person. And yet, a confession is without effect unless it is confessed by a person, and so the Fathers also identify the Roman See in a particular way with this promise (in addition to every bishop in a different sense).[10]

One of most famous instances of this is the formula of Hormisdas. This was the confession which ended the Acacian schism, the first prolonged east-west schism. It lasted nearly two generations from 484-519. The confession reads like this:

> The first condition of salvation is to keep the norm of the true faith and in no way to deviate from the established doctrine of the Fathers. For it is impossible that the words of our Lord Jesus Christ, who said, "Thou art Peter, and upon this rock I will build my Church," should not be verified. And their truth has been proved by the course of history, for in the Apostolic See the Catholic religion has always been kept

---

succession, the office of the first true believer, Peter." John Meyendorff, *The Primacy of Peter*, (Crestwood, NY: St. Vladimir's Seminary Press, 1992), 89.
[9] See E. Ybarra, "Pope Victor I (189-98) & the Roman Primacy – Critical Analysis," (Jan. 13, 2017), <https://erickybarra.wordpress.com/2017/01/13/pope-victor-i-189-98-the-roman-primacy-critical-analysis/>, accessed October 23, 2023.
[10] For the latest scholarship on this question, see E. Ybarra, *The Papacy* (St. Paul Center, 2023).

unsullied. [Here follows a list of condemned heretics.]

Following, as we have said before, the Apostolic See in all things and proclaiming all its decisions, we endorse and approve all the letters which Pope St Leo wrote concerning the Christian religion. *And so I hope I may deserve to be associated with you in the one communion which the Apostolic See proclaims, in which the whole, true, and perfect security of the Christian religion resides.* I promise that from now on those who are separated from the communion of the Catholic Church, that is, who are not in agreement with the Apostolic See, will not have their names read during the sacred mysteries. But if I attempt even the least deviation from my profession, I admit that, according to my own declaration, I am an accomplice to those whom I have condemned. I have signed this, my profession, with my own hand, and I have directed it to you, Hormisdas, the holy and venerable pope of Rome.

This confession formed the basis for reunion with the Church of two thousand five hundred Eastern schismatic bishops in 519. It was invoked again at the Ecumenical Council in 869 and again at Florence in the 15th century. The documentary evidence for Rome's special place in this promise is evident for those who have eyes to see.

The important point we wish to draw out here is the adjoining verses about "Satan." Because although it is clear that the Pope of Rome has from the earliest times been the point of infallible unity, it is also true that the popes have lapsed into error of various kinds as we have already mentioned.[11] Perhaps this is why Our Lord, after His majestic exaltation of St. Peter on the mountain, quickly rebukes him when he denies the cross and calls him "Satan." We may infer from these passages that Our Lord does indeed promise the indestructability of St. Peter and His Church, but he does not promise impeccability of the Roman Pontiff.

In other words, His promise will be fulfilled, one way or another, but this does not personally force the will of the pope (or any bishop) to be without sin and error. The pope retains his free will. Insofar as he confesses the faith that his name bears, he unites his person and the Church with the rock of truth. This, of course, is the work of God's grace and Providence, and is not ascribed to his human will. Our Lord has promised that this rock will never truly be shaken, *even if it is completely killed* as He Himself was.

On the other hand, insofar as the person of St. Peter according to his human nature denies the cross of suffering, he becomes Satan. Solovyov summarizes this beautifully when he says:

> Simon Peter as supreme pastor and doctor of the Universal Church, assisted by God and speaking in the name of all, is the faithful witness and infallible exponent of divine-human truth; as such he is the impregnable foundation of the house of God and the key-bearer of the Kingdom of Heaven. The same Simon Peter as a private individual, speaking and acting by his natural powers and merely human intelligence, may say and do things that are unworthy, scandalous and even diabolical. But the failures and sins of the individual are

---

[11] Peter Kwasniewski, "Lessons from Church History: A Brief Review of Papal Lapses," *OnePeterFive* (Aug 6, 2018) <https://onepeterfive.com/lessons-church-history-papal-lapses/>, accessed October 23, 2023.

ephemeral, while the social function of the ecclesiastical monarch is permanent. "Satan" and the "offence" have vanished, but Peter has remained.[12]

Thus "Satan" and "Rock" are two names for the Apostle, yet not in the same way. Rock ("Peter") is according to God's grace and providence, Satan is according to Simon's own frail human nature. From a purely human perspective, the gates of hell do prevail in this sense, but not from the perspective of God. Man can truly see the triumph of Hell according to his eyes of flesh. Considering the death of Our Lord, we must expect the most awful tragedy imaginable to overcome the Roman Church, so that it becomes *absolutely impossible* for the Church to survive. Only then can we look for the glorious resurrection. Only then can God receive all glory. As it is written, *Power is made perfect in infirmity* (II Cor. xii. 9) and again, *What is impossible for man is possible with God* (Lk xviii. 27).

Our fathers have indeed seen the gates of hell prevail with their natural eyes. They have seen the papacy overrun by heretics. Destroyed by pagans and Iconoclasts. They have seen the popes murdered, or the popes as murderers and adulterers. They have seen the pope teach heresy, order public debauchery and toast Satan. The eyes of the flesh see that this is the gates of hell prevailing. But the eyes of faith see what is unseen. As St. Paul says, *faith is the substance of things to be hoped for, the evidence of things that appear not* (Heb. xi. 1).

In the midst of crises in Church history, our fathers were willing to shed their blood for these awful popes. St. Thomas More was beheaded for a pope with mistresses and multiple illegitimate children. The Japanese Church endured two hundred years without priests, keeping the faith. Although they could see that the gates of hell were indeed prevailing,

---

[12] Vladimir Solovyov, *Russia and the Universal Church*, trans. Rees (London: Centenary Press, 1948), 92.

their faith told them that whatever happens, they will not prevail in the end. This is the reasoning of faith.

As we have seen, the Fathers and saints have never defined exactly what the triumph of the gates of hell means. With the death of the Son of God, all manner of evil done to the Church is foreshadowed. It has not been revealed to us in what way the gates of hell could prevail, we have only been promised that they will not prevail in the end.

We must have the faith of Abraham who believed that God would raise up seed for him even though he was as good as dead (Heb. xi. 12). Then we must be willing to sacrifice that seed in faith, reasoning through faith that God would reconcile the former promise of seed and the present command to sacrifice–only by raising the dead back to life (Heb. xi. 19). Faith and hope will deliver us through this crisis, as they delivered our fathers.

"The Church is a perpetually defeated thing that always outlives her conquerors." — Hilaire Belloc

Dogmas of Indefectibility and the Wrath of God

Finally, we must consider the dogma of the wrath of God and balance this with the doctrine of the indefectibility of the Church. What is the doctrine of the wrath of God? Consider II Macc. vi. 12-15:

> Now I beseech those that shall read this book, that they be not shocked at these calamities, but that they consider the things that happened, not as being for the destruction, but for the correction of our nation. For it is a token of great goodness when sinners are not suffered to go on in their ways for a long time, but are presently punished. For, not as with other nations (whom the Lord patiently expecteth, that when the day of judgment shall come, he may punish them in the fulness of their sins:)

Doth he also deal with us, so as to suffer our sins to come to their height, and then take vengeance on us.

Let us not be shocked by the calamities of the Church. It is the wrath of God to punish and cleanse the Church. Not for her destruction, but for her correction. *But esteeming these very punishments to be less than our sins deserve, let us believe that these scourges of the Lord, with which like servants we are chastised, have happened for our amendment, and not for our destruction* (Judith viii. 27). And the saints offer up penance that *in me and in my brethren the wrath of the Almighty, which hath justly been brought upon all our nation, shall cease* (II Macc. vii. 38).

Therefore we know that the Church will not be destroyed, but in the wrath of God, we also know that she will look like she is destroyed. This consideration should guide us to greater penance. What do Catholics do in dark times? *Penance. Penance. Penance.*

This leads us to the dogma of the indefectibility of the Church, which must be balanced with the former. This is the same doctrine we have been discussing which comes from the promise of Christ about the gates of Hell.

As we said, the doctrine does not have a lot of specific content other than this general promise which we can take to the extreme. In researching this dogma of indefectability I consulted with a number of theologians. They confirmed to me that the dogma itself is rather minimal in its specifics. Here's my question to one theologian summarizing this dogma:

> **Flanders:** The question is this: given that the indefectability of the Church is De Fide, what would need to happen for this dogma to be falsified?
>
> It seems that the specifics of the dogma have not been very much defined. What really has

36

been definitively established about what this looks like?

It seems only some general very minimal things – that the Church cannot cease to be "one [unity somewhere with the bishop of Rome], Holy [dispense Sacramental Grace ordinarily], Catholic [the Faith will always exist somewhere], and Apostolic [even if the pope utterly fails, the Papacy will somehow endure as the Rock at least in potency].

Dr. John Joy: Yes, it's fairly minimal. The Church will always remain the Church. Nothing essential to her nature or existence will perish from her. That means the Apostolic succession will not be broken, the sacraments will not utterly disappear, and error in faith or morals will not be definitively taught. There will be a Pope, even if not always a good one. The Church still existed on Holy Saturday when all but our Lady had lost the faith.

Dr. Joy, while not intending here to make an exhaustive statement, nevertheless summarizes the dogma as a minimum of definitive claims. In other words, the Magisterium has not definitively decided many different aspects of this dogma, other than various general promises.

I spoke to another theologian of the Magisterium, Dr. Mike Sirilla, who defined the dogma like this:

Dr. Mike Sirilla: Indefectability means that the essential features of the Church remain in an unbroken chain until the end of time. The essential features are: the same faith, the same sacraments, and the hierarchical structure of governance established by Christ. Minimally only one valid bishop and one Catholic who professed the true faith is required. That one bishop could become the bishop of Rome and continue the papacy and consecrate new bishops.

So again there's a minimum required for this dogma, and it seems the crisis could get a whole lot worse and the dogma would still be preserved. Still, in the period following Vatican I, many theologians had an exalted view of this dogma, so that sometimes there were speculations that went beyond this minimum.

Lay people who are not trained in all these difficult speculations should not worry too much about them – our forefathers certainly did not, and they went on passing down to us the Faith in which we now stand. As for us, we can have hope in the promise of Our Lord, even if He does not give us the clear, definitive answers we want to hear. But this is a test of our faith. Let us walk by faith, and not by sight.

In short, let's expect the worst and hope for the best.

III

The Last Christian on Earth

Friday has always been a day of penance for the universal Church, commemorating the blessed Passion of Our Lord.[13] Sunday is *"the Lord's Day"* (Apoc. i. 10), the day of the Holy Sacrifice of the Mass – commemorating, together with Calvary, Our Lord's glorious Resurrection. In the Latin Church, the custom is well established to dedicate Saturday to Our Lady as a special commemoration.[14]

This custom seems to have originated in the 10th century. During this era, the Church in the West suffered under what is known as the *saeculum obscurum* ("dark age"). Impious and wicked Roman nobility held power over the papacy as a pawn of their own ambitions. It was the era of the infamous Pope John XII (r. 955-964), whom St. Robert Bellarmine (1542-1621) called "practically the worst of all pontiffs."[15]

In this dark time, the stalwart monks of Cluny began the reform which eventually took back the Papacy for Christ, cleansing the Church of the dominion of filth. It was a major figure of this salutary reform, St. Hugh of Cluny (1024-1109), who spread the Saturday Marian devotion. Special Saturday Mass propers for Our Lady can be found in the Leofric Missal

---

[13] Cf. *Didache*, ch. 8.

[14] In the East, Saturday is dedicated as a memorial for the dead, commemorating Our Lord "sleeping" in the tomb.

[15] *Omnium pontificum fere deterrimus. De Romano Pontifice*, l. II, ch. 19. See Roberto de Mattei, "Who Was the Worst Pope in the History of the Church?" *Corrispondenza Romana* (December 4th, 2019) trans. Francesca Romana <https://rorate-caeli.blogspot.com/2019/12/de-mattei-who-was-worst-pope-in-history.html>, accessed March 16, 2021.

which dates to this period.[16] The custom of the Saturday Marian devotion spread in conjunction with the Cluniac reform, causing a lasting impact on popular devotion and the sacred rites of the Church.

In rubrics for the 1962 Missal, the Mass for Our Lady is said on every Saturday which is IV class, as is the Office of Our Lady in the Benedictine and Roman Breviaries. In other words, Mary is commemorated on every Saturday outside Lent and Advent, unless superseded by some other feast.

Why is Mary Commemorated on Saturday?

The origins and reasons for this custom remain somewhat obscure from a historical perspective.[17] However, the time of the Cluniac effort against the darkness of that time corresponds to the meaning popularly given to Mary's veneration on Saturday in particular.

Here we recall Holy Week and find a most salutary devotion in the Marian Office of Saturday, especially for our times. As we said in the last chatper, let's consider for a moment the scene of Holy Saturday in the Upper Room and the events of the previous day. Our Blessed Lord has been crucified and laid in the tomb. Despite their solemn assurances that they were ready to die with Him (Matt. xxvi. 35), all of His Apostles fled at the time of His arrest in the Garden of Gethsemane (Mk. xiv. 48-53), although Sts. Peter and John followed at a safe distance afterward (Jn. xviii. 15-16). The Prince of the Apostles denied his Lord (Lk. xxii. 55-62) and one of the Twelve, Judas the betrayer, killed himself (Mt. xxvii. 3-5). The Romans hold power and the Jewish temple guards patrol the tomb. *Jesus Christ is dead.* The disciples hide *for fear of the Jews* (Jn. xx. 19), weighed down by the shame

---

[16] The earliest instance of this, however, is found in a Missal from Alcuin of York (d. 804): *Le sacramentaire grégorien*, II, ed. J. Deshusses, *Editions Universitaires* (Fribourg 1988), pp. 25-27 and 45; PL 101, 455-456.

[17] Umberto de Romanis, *De vita regulari* II, Ch. 24.

of their own betrayal while their hope has evaporated. Now all hope is lost and darkness covers the earth.

Think of a time when you felt like despairing. I assure you, their despair was worse.

All the followers of the would-be Messiah now sit and mourn. They *mourn as those who have no hope* (I Thess. iv. 13). It is the Sabbath observance of resting from work. But their strength has left them (Ps. xxxviii. 11) and they water their bed with tears (Ps. vi. 7). They now slumber from despondency (Ps. cxviii. 28) and cry out: *Lord, where are Thy ancient mercies, according to what Thou didst swear to David in Thy truth?* (Ps. lxxxviii. 50). On this Saturday, all the faithful have lost hope.

All save one. Mary, Our Lady. Our Queen and Mother. She is the one who never lost hope on that Saturday. She never failed to maintain hope in the prophetic words of her Divine Son and Lord: *For He shall be delivered to the Gentiles and shall be mocked and scourged and spit upon. And after they have scourged Him, they will put Him to death. And the third day He shall rise again* (Lk. xviii. 32-33).

On that day, she was the last Christian on earth.

The Saturday Office of Mary commemorates Our Lady's hope when all hope was gone. When silence gripped the earth as it shuddered with horror (Jer. ii. 12) at the death of Christ (Mt. xxvii. 50-51) and everywhere there was a darkness that could be felt (Ex. x. 21). But Mary held fast to *the light [that] shineth in darkness* (Jn. i. 5). She alone kept in her heart the most impossible hope in the face of the finality of death. She alone understood and believed: *With men this is impossible: but with God all things are possible* (Mt. xix. 26). This is the reason for her Saturday memorial.

Thus, we see the connection between Our Lady's indomitable hope on Holy Saturday and the Cluniac monks of the *saeculum obscurum* ("dark age") who established Saturday as devoted to Our Lady. This is the lesson of the Saturday Office. If there was ever a time at which all hope seemed certainly lost, it was at the death of Jesus Christ. And so, in every era from that time forward when it seems all hope was lost, this Saturday Office makes us remember what Our Lady did when she faced the death of God Himself.

"Yes, God is dead"—she herself laid Him in the tomb with a sorrow that no man has ever known—"but He will rise again." She had hope in the promise. They must have thought her crazy, but she held on to this hope.

Her whole life, she knew the reality of the Son of God Who was born from her, conceived of the Holy Ghost; when the Angel had promised that *the Lord God shall give unto Him the throne of David His father: and He shall reign in the house of Jacob forever. And of His kingdom there shall be no end* (Lk. i. 32). Now, in the face of the death of her Son the King, she still believed. Like Abraham (Heb. xi. 19), she reasoned that God would raise the dead, as He had said.

The Saturday Office is a commemoration of the infallible hope of Our Lady. It was the perfect custom to galvanize the Cluniac monks of the 10th and 11th centuries in the face of a corrupted Church hierarchy. As such, it is also fitting for our time, now further exalted by Our Lady of Fatima—but we will return to this below.

Her hope came from the promises of God. It came from a faith that He is God and He will be faithful to what He says He will do. It was Mary who had faith, as the Holy Ghost had declared through St. Elizabeth: "And blessed art thou that hast believed, because those things shall be accomplished that were spoken to thee by the Lord" (Lk. 1:45).

The Saturday Office and Hope

St. Thomas Aquinas explains the relationship between faith and hope:

> [F]aith precedes hope. For the object of hope is
> a future good, arduous but possible to obtain.
> In order, therefore, that we may hope, it is
> necessary for the object of hope to be proposed

42

to us as possible. Now the object of hope is, in one way, eternal happiness, and in another way, the Divine assistance... and both of these are proposed to us by faith, whereby we come to know that we are able to obtain eternal life, and that for this purpose the Divine assistance is ready for us, according to Heb. 11:6: *He that cometh to God, must believe that He is, and is a rewarder to them that seek Him* (II-II q7 a7).

Thus, we say that the promises of God were given to Mary as something that God intended to accomplish. These promises were accepted on faith. We then have hope in the divine power to accomplish that which was promised. This is the soft rebuke of the Angel to the disciples: *He is risen, as He said* (Mt. xxviii. 6).

St. Thomas says the motive of hope is the power of God, whereas other theologians identify the goodness of God or His faithfulness as grounds for hope.[18] But we see above, the primary object of hope is eternal happiness in God. We hope in God for His assistance to bring us to eternal life, just as Our Lady hoped for the Resurrection. Fr. Dominic M. Prümmer, O.P. elaborates in his classic work, *Handbook of Moral Theology*:

> Hope is steadfast, in so far as it is based on the help of God; there is, however, some fear and uncertainty in the virtue inasmuch as it supposes our own co-operation. It is evident from the words of the Council of Trent that hope is completely steadfast: 'Everyone must place and put the most steadfast hope in the help of God' (Sess. 6, c. 13 *De Justif.*). However, Sacred Scripture points to the uncertainty and fear present in hope because of

---

[18] Prümmer identifies the Scotists and Suárez as other theologians here. *Handbook of Moral Theology* (Roman Catholic Books: 1957), no. 209.

man's uncertain co-operation: *Man does not know whether he is deserving of love or of hatred* (Eccles. 9:1).[19]

Here arises the spiritual axiom from Dom Lorenzo Scupoli, author of *The Spiritual Combat*, which is fundamental to the spiritual life: distrust of self, and trust in God.

> Distrust of self is so absolutely requisite in the spiritual combat, that without this virtue we cannot expect to defeat our weakest passions, much less gain a complete victory. This important truth should be deeply imbedded in our hearts; for, although in ourselves we are nothing, we are too apt to overestimate our own abilities and to conclude falsely that we are of some importance. This vice springs from the corruption of our nature. But the more natural a thing is, the more difficult it is to be discovered.

> But God, to Whom nothing is secret, looks upon this with horror, because it is His Will that we should be convinced we possess only that virtue and grace which comes from Him alone, and that without Him we are incapable of one meritorious thought. This distrust of our own strength is a gift from Heaven, bestowed by God on those He loves.[20]

It was this important truth which was deeply imbedded in the Immaculate Heart of the Virgin Mary: *without Me, you can do nothing* (Jn. xv. 5). This is why she was the most humble of all creatures and thus was able to accomplish the will of God. On Holy Saturday, it was her hope which carried the

---

[19] Ibid.
[20] Dom Scupoli, *The Spiritual Combat*, ch. 2.

entire Church. She knew that by her own power, or any human power, the Resurrection was impossible. In the same way, when we consider our own soul in regard to eternal life, we must know that *of our own strength, salvation is impossible.*

But Scupoli continues and contrasts the distrust of self with the trust in God:

> Although distrust of self is absolutely necessary... nevertheless, if this is all we have to rely on, we will soon be routed, plundered, and subdued by the enemy. Unless we would be put to flight, or remain helpless and vanquished in the hands of our enemies, we must add to it *perfect trust in God,* and expect from Him alone succor and victory. For as we, who are nothing, can look for nothing from ourselves but falls, and therefore should utterly distrust ourselves; so from Our Lord may we *assuredly expect complete victory in every conflict.* To obtain His help, let us therefore arm ourselves with a lively confidence in Him.[21]

Here we understand the saying of Our Lord that with man these things are impossible, but they are possible with God. We must not have any hope in ourselves to accomplish anything, nor in the power of man. *Put not your trust in princes: in the children of men, in whom there is no salvation* (Ps. cxlv. 2-3). But our hope in God must be confident and steadfast, as was Our Lady's hope. She hoped in the complete victory of Christ. This is our struggle in the spiritual life, and we can find no greater example than what the Saturday Memorial of Our Lady commemorates.

---

[21] Ibid., Ch. 3. Emphasis mine.

The Saturday Memorial Against Despair

In our times, many souls despair and lose hope, just as the disciples did on Holy Saturday. It is important to remember that despair is a sin. St. Thomas says that despair is a sin and the origin of sins, quoting Ephesians: *Who despairing have given themselves up to lasciviousness, unto the working of all uncleanness, unto covetousness* (iv. 19). He elaborates on the relationship between faith and hope in the sin of despair, showing that it stems from an error in faith:

> [T]ruth and falsehood in the intellect correspond to good and evil in the appetite. Consequently, every appetitive movement which is conformed to a true intellect is good in itself, while every appetitive movement which is conformed to a false intellect is evil in itself and sinful.

> Now the true opinion of the intellect about God is that from Him comes salvation to mankind, and pardon to sinners, according to Ezech. 18:23, *I desire not the death of the sinner, but that he should be converted, and live*: while it is a false opinion that He refuses pardon to the repentant sinner, or that He does not turn sinners to Himself by sanctifying grace.

> Therefore, just as the movement of hope, which is in conformity with the true opinion, is praiseworthy and virtuous, so the contrary movement of despair, which is in conformity with the false opinion about God, is vicious and sinful (II-II q20 a1).

Mary believed the word that was spoken to her, and this became the foundation of her hope. But a soul may disbelieve the words of God, which leads him descending into despair. This is what Scupoli said above: if we rely *only* on our distrust of self, then we "remain helpless and vanquished in the hands of our enemies." Our distrust of ourselves, based on the truth about our capacity without grace, must then be matched and exceeded by an ever greater hope in God—the truth of faith. Therefore, as St. Thomas indicates, we must fight despair by identifying the central error in our faith which is leading us to a "false opinion about God."

Would Mary have ever entertained a doubt on Holy Saturday that Our Lord would not rise as He said? Never! This would be a false opinion about God. *God is not a man, that He should lie: nor as the son of man, that He should be changed. Hath He said then, and will He not do? Hath He spoken, and will He not fulfill?* (Num. xxiii. 19).

What are the false opinions about God that are polluting your faith? What doubts are arising in your soul as you struggle to face the reality of the crisis in the Church and the world? Turn to Mary Most Holy, the Virgin most faithful, and ask her to obtain the grace of hope for you against despair. Remember the promises of our Blessed Lord. Consider how she hoped against hope, when all hope seemed lost. Her hope became the whole foundation of the Church.

The First Saturdays Devotion

Just over one hundred years ago, Our Lady of Fatima came to sanctify the Saturday Memorial with the First Saturdays devotion. During her third apparition (July 13, 1917), when millions of bodies lay dead during the First World War, she told the three shepherd children:

> If what I say to you is done, many souls will be saved and there will be peace. The war is going to end: but if people do not cease offending God, a worse one will break out during the Pontificate of Pius XI. When you see a night

illumined by an unknown light, know that this is the great sign given you by God that he is about to punish the world for its crimes, by means of war, famine, and persecutions of the Church and of the Holy Father. To prevent this, I shall come to ask for the consecration of Russia to my Immaculate Heart, and the Communion of reparation on the First Saturdays.

It was indeed a time of great despair and darkness. But as she promised, Our Lady returned in 1925 and told Lucia, the eldest of the three seers who had since entered religious life:

Look, my daughter, at my Heart, surrounded with thorns with which ungrateful men pierce me at every moment by their blasphemies and ingratitude. You at least try to console me and announce in my name that I promise to assist at the moment of death, with all the graces necessary for salvation, all those who, on the first Saturday of five consecutive months shall receive the sacrament of Confession, receive Holy Communion, recite five decades of the Rosary, and keep me company for fifteen minutes while meditating on the fifteen mysteries of the Rosary, with the intention of making reparation to my Immaculate Heart.[22]

In these respective messages, we see two amazing promises from Our Lady: one for world peace, the other for final perseverance at the hour of death. Men did not repent, and God's wrath was poured out in World War II. However, her promise "to assist at the moment of death" all souls who

---

[22] "The Apparitions at Pontevedra (1925-1926)," *The Fatima Center* <https://fatima.org/about/fatima-the-facts/the-apparitions-at-pontevedra>, accessed October 23, 2023.

are faithful to her "with all the graces necessary for salvation" remains. Moreover, she also made this promise: "In the end, my Immaculate Heart will triumph." It is this same Immaculate Heart which ever hoped in the promise of God. Her triumph shall be the triumph of Our Lord, just as He rose from the dead. So too will His intervention be the triumph of Our Lady. For her hope was vindicated at the Resurrection, just as her promise at Fatima will be vindicated when the Lord acts with His almighty power.

Let us meditate on Saturdays on Our Lady's indomitable hope. As St. Paul says:

> Being justified therefore by faith, let us have peace with God, through our Lord Jesus Christ: By Whom also we have access through faith into this grace, wherein we stand, and glory in the hope of the glory of the sons of God. And not only so; but we glory also in tribulations, knowing that tribulation worketh patience; and patience trial; and trial hope; and hope confoundeth not: because the charity of God is poured forth in our hearts, by the Holy Ghost Who is given to us (Rom. v. 1-5).

IV

Christ Crucified: God's Answer to the Problem of Suffering

The problem of suffering is the problem that every human movement is trying to resolve. It is at the heart of the deepest questions that man can ask and with which man can struggle. St. Thomas Aquinas identifies this as one of the only arguments that can be made against the existence of God:

> Objection: It seems that God does not exist; because if there are two contrary things and one is infinite, the other would be totally destroyed. But the word 'God' means that He is infinite goodness. If, therefore, God existed, there would not be any evil to be found; but there is evil in the world. Therefore, God does not exist (I q2 a3).[23]

Man encounters suffering and must find a way to resolve this tension that he feels between the way things are, the way they make him feel, and the way he thinks they ought to be. In his despair, he may turn to Agnosticism or Atheism, or he may embrace various false gospels.

Buddhists proclaim their false gospel of *nirvana*, or nothingness, in which all suffering is absent because there is

---

[23] Translation my own. *Videtur quod Deus non sit. Quia si unum contrariorum fuerit infinitum, totaliter destruetur aliud. Sed hoc intelligitur in hoc nomine Deus, scilicet quod sit quoddam bonum infinitum. Si ergo Deus esset, nullum malum inveniretur. Invenitur autem malum in mundo. Ergo Deus non est.*

nothing. Muhammadans proclaim their false gospel of submission to a false god and his false prophet. This god is too transcendent to be a Father or a God of love, and thus suffering is ultimately what their false god wills. But these false gospels ultimately flee from the problem of suffering by trying to ignore the painful issue, hoping it will go away.

The currently dominant false gospel of psychology (first popularized in the 1960s during the Human Potential Movement and Sexual Revolution) proclaims the errors of Sigmund Freud and Wilhelm Reich. They say that suffering is a result of failing to let your emotions out, or repressing your inner desires. The false gospel of psychology, in particular, is the one that has overtaken the Church in our time, as they have stripped the Sacred Liturgy of everything that does not make people "feel good," and many clergy are more concerned with making people "feel good" than preaching the hard truths of the Gospel and repentance.[24] Even worse, many men have identified the charity and mercy of Jesus Christ particularly with this false "niceness" and "feelings." But this, again, simply buries the problem of suffering in a distraction of positive emotions. The problem of suffering will always return, no matter how effective a false gospel may be in causing a prolonged distraction.

The True Gospel of Christ Crucified

None of these false gospels will ever answer the problem of suffering because they fail to give the answer revealed by

---

[24] This was Bugnini's famous justification for gutting the liturgy of our fathers so that Protestants would feel welcome: "We must strip from our liturgies everything that would be a shadow of a stumbling block to Protestants" (March 19, 1965 edition of *L'Osservatore Romano*). In the same way, the post-conciliar Liturgy of the Hours (Divine Office) specifically justifies their censoring of certain Psalm verses and entire Psalms for "psychological" reasons (*General Instruction of the Liturgy of the Hours*, 131). Finally, in the new lectionary, "texts that present real difficulties are avoided for pastoral reasons" (*General Introduction to the Lectionary*, 76).

God Himself. No man can resolve this problem without God's help. St. Thomas gives the answer to the objection given above:

> As Augustine says (Enchiridion xi): 'Since God is the highest good, He would not allow any evil to exist in His works, unless His omnipotence and goodness were such as to bring good even out of evil.' This is part of the infinite goodness of God, that He should allow evil to exist, and out of it produce good (I q2 a3 ad1).

God demonstrates His infinite goodness and omnipotence in that He produces good even out of evil and suffering. Against the raucous din of the false gospels trying in vain to overcome the problem of suffering, the Church solemnly proclaims the good news of truth to every creature under heaven:

> *Ecce lignum Crucis, in quo salus mundi pepéndit.*
> *Veníte, adorémus.*
>
> Behold, the wood of the Cross, on which hung the salvation of the world.
> Come, let us adore.[25]

It is in Christ Crucified that the problem of suffering is forever answered. This is the true Gospel, which enters into the heart of man and the darkness of his evil and suffering:

> But we preach Christ crucified, unto the Jews indeed a stumbling block, and unto the Gentiles foolishness: But unto them that are called, both

---

[25] Antiphon at the Elevation of the Cross, Good Friday Liturgy.

Jews and Greeks, Christ the power of God, and
the wisdom of God. For the foolishness of God
is wiser than men; and the weakness of God is
stronger than men (I Cor. i. 23-25).

This is the infinite goodness of God in that "He should
allow evil to exist, and out of it produce good." There is no
greater good for man than the eternal salvation of souls. And
this was accomplished out of the gravest evil imaginable: the
brutal crucifixion and ignominious death of the sinless Son of
God—the Cross. Every Christian venerates this symbol of
salvation, which has been transformed from a symbol of evil.
Before the Cross of Christ, this instrument of torture and death
stood for fear and domination to all who saw it. Now, this
symbol is lifted before the faithful, kindling charity in their
hearts. It is lifted before the pagans, preaching the Gospel of
their salvation from idols. It is lifted before the Jews and
Muhammadans, calling them to baptism and eternal life. Who
cannot marvel at the infinite goodness of God, bringing His
greatest good for man out of such a horrific evil?

The Cross of Suffering for Every Christian

Therefore, the Church rejoices in the suffering of Jesus
Christ her Savior:

We adore Thy Cross, O Lord: and we praise and glorify
Thy holy resurrection: for behold by the wood of the
Cross joy came into the whole world.[26]

The Cross is venerated as the means of our salvation. It is
honored as the instrument of suffering by which the world is
saved from eternal damnation. This is the infinite goodness of
God in bringing the greatest good out of the evil of crucifixion.

---

[26] Antiphon before the *Crux Fidelis*, Good Friday Liturgy.

But this is not the false gospel of Luther and the Protestants, wherein this Cross is celebrated, yet our lives are not truly impacted. The true Gospel of Jesus Christ makes the Cross penetrate the very soul of the Christian, so that his sufferings too are united to the Cross of Christ. As the Apostle declares: *I now rejoice in my sufferings for you, and fill up those things that are wanting of the sufferings of Christ, in my flesh, for his body, which is the church* (Col. i. 24).

The Protestant cannot understand this verse because it runs contrary to their false gospel. But Augustine explains:

> He did not say "of the sufferings of me" but "of Christ," because he was a member of Christ and in His persecutions, such as it was necessary for Christ to suffer in His whole body, even Paul was filling up Christ's affliction in Paul's own portion.[27]

Christ, Who has ascended to heaven, *dieth no more* (Rom. vi. 9), yet the Christian can say with St. Paul, *I die daily* (I Cor. xv. 31) and again *Always bearing about in our body the mortification of Jesus, that the life also of Jesus may be made manifest in our bodies* (II Cor. iv. 10). Christ as head of the Church, does not suffer any more in heaven. And yet the Church as His Body and each of us as His members indeed suffer here on earth, and these sufferings are not our own, but also Christ's. This is the reason that Our Lord could say to St. Paul before His conversion: *Saul, Saul, why dost thou persecute me?* (Acts ix. 4). Christ, says Augustine in another place, speaks and identifies Himself with His Body no less than He does with His Head—Christ is not divided, but one person.[28] Each of us has our "own portion" of Christ's sufferings to bear here on earth.

---

[27] St. Augustine, *Tractates on the Gospel of John: 55-111* (CUA Press: 1994), 282.
[28] St. Augustine, *Commentary on the Psalms, Ps. 37.*

Understand then, O Christian, how noble, true and good can be your sufferings. Christ Himself will deign to make these sufferings His own, if only you, through His grace, unite yourself to Him. Do not scorn your sufferings as so many discomforts and annoyances, but as you venerate the Cross of Christ so offer your own sufferings in imitation of and union with Him. Fr. Reginald Garrigou-Lagrange, O.P. (1877-1964), one of the greatest theologians and spiritual masters of the 20th century, wrote concerning this subject:

> This spirit of detachment through imitation of Jesus crucified... is the condition of a close union with God, whence supernatural life overflows in a manner ever new, and at times stupendous, for the eternal welfare of souls. This is evidenced by the lives of all the saints without exception, and we ought to nourish our souls daily with the examples of these great servants of God. The world is not so much in need of philosophers and sociologists, as of saints who are the living image of the Savior among us.[29]

Thus, we see that the Cross not only saves us from eternal damnation but also becomes the means by which we enter into "a close union with God," by accepting our share in the sufferings of His Son. This is where salutary suffering begins to transform the individual soul.

Christ Commands the Christian to Suffer with Him

The Imitation of Christ by Thomas à Kempis (d. 1471) speaks profoundly on this point:

---

[29] Fr. Reginald Garrigou-Lagrange, O.P., *The Three Ages of the Spiritual Life* Vol. I (Herder: 1947), p. 297.

To many the saying, *Deny thyself, take up thy cross and follow Me* (Mt. xvi. 24), seems hard, but it will be much harder to hear that final word: *Depart from Me, ye cursed, into everlasting fire* (Mt. xxv. 41). Those who hear the word of the cross and follow it willingly now, need not fear that they will hear of eternal damnation on the day of judgment. This sign of the cross will be in the heavens when the Lord comes to judge. Then all the servants of the cross, who during life made themselves one with the Crucified, will draw near with great trust to Christ, the Judge[.]

...How is it that you look for another way than this, the royal way of the holy cross? The whole life of Christ was a cross and a martyrdom, and do you seek rest and enjoyment for yourself? You deceive yourself, you are mistaken if you seek anything but to suffer, for this mortal life is full of miseries and marked with crosses on all sides. Indeed, the more spiritual progress a person makes, so much heavier will he frequently find the cross, because as his love increases, the pain of his exile also increases.

Yet such a man, though afflicted in many ways, is not without hope of consolation, because he knows that great reward is coming to him for bearing his cross. And when he carries it willingly, every pang of tribulation is changed into hope of solace from God. Besides, the more the flesh is distressed by affliction, so much the more is the spirit strengthened by inward grace. Not infrequently a man is so strengthened by his love of trials and hardship in his desire to conform to the cross of Christ, that he does not wish to be without sorrow or pain, since he believes he will be the more acceptable to God if he is able to endure more and more grievous things for His sake. It is the grace of Christ, and not the virtue of man, which can and does bring it about that through fervor of spirit frail flesh learns to love and to gain what it naturally hates and shuns.[30]

The pious soul will long to be united to Jesus Christ in His Passion, for as the charity of a soul increases, so does the love of suffering which conforms a soul to Christ. But this starts with the very command of Christ to partake of His cross with Him. Fr. Ignatius of the Side of Jesus contemplates this reality in the person of Simon of Cyrene:

[Jesus'] consent that another should relieve Him of His Cross arises from no desire of unburdening His sacred shoulders, but is a mystery intended to teach us that He is pleased to share His sufferings with all His elect. On the other hand, Jesus is, at the same time, ready to bear His Cross so long as to fall several times beneath its weight, and even finally to expire upon it. And with what degree of constancy do you bear your Cross? Do you persevere in virtue? Are you firm and constant in your resolution to follow Jesus Christ, and to suffer with Him and for Him? Remember that whoever does not take up his Cross and follow Jesus is not worthy of Him. Whoever has not partaken of His sufferings will not partake of His glory. Jesus desires to associate us with Himself in His eternal happiness, and for that

---

[30] Thomas à Kempis, *The Imitation of Christ*, Bk II, ch. 12.

reason it is His will that we, in the person of
Simon of Cyrene, should assist Him to carry
His Cross.[31]

Therefore, we must be assured that Our Lord not only
procures our salvation with His Holy Cross, but also
commands us to partake of this suffering with Him, in order
that our sufferings too will be transformed by the infinite
goodness of God. Herein we will find union with our Savior.

Original Sin and Attachment

But how does God transform our sufferings into union with
Him? We must understand our condition to understand the
salutary good in suffering. We are afflicted with the effects of
Original Sin: a darkened intellect, weakened will, and a heart
inclined to evil. In particular, this is seen in our attachments to
created things. An attachment may be defined as a strong or
even overwhelming inclination toward something which pulls
your intellect and will like gravity. In modern usage, we might
also use the word "addiction." These can be unlawful
pleasures, such as sins against the Sixth Commandment, but
they can also be lawful pleasures, like food and drink,
entertainment, or social media. Even more, the saints tell us,
we can become attached to very good things like consolations
and joys, whether natural or supernatural. All of these
excessive attachments, however, incline our hearts away from
the only place where attachment should be: God alone. As
Thomas à Kempis teaches in *The Imitation of Christ*:

> Unless a man be disengaged from all things
> created, he cannot freely attend to things
> divine[.]... And unless a man be elevated in
> spirit, and free from attachment to all creatures,

---

[31] Fr. Ignatius of the Side of Jesus, *The School of Jesus Crucified* (1866),
Day 23.

and wholly united to God, whatever he knows and whatever he has is of no great importance.[32]

Sufferings must be embraced because they break the cycle of attachment that we have to created things, giving us an occasion to unite ourselves to God more closely. Here we can begin to develop the spirit of detachment from what is created, in order to attach ourselves to the Uncreated. Fr. Garrigou-Lagrange elaborates:

> We should detach ourselves from exterior goods, riches and honors. *If riches abound, set not your heart upon them* (Ps. lxi. 11). St. Paul says: *The time is short ... and they that rejoice, as if they rejoiced not; ... and they that use this world, as if they used it not* (I Cor. vii. 29-31). Even those who do not effectively practice the counsel of evangelical poverty ought to have its spirit if they wish to tend to perfection.

> We must detach ourselves from the goods of the body, from beauty, from health itself; it would be an aberration to cling to them more than to union with God. And we cling to health far more than we think; if it were irremediably taken from us, it would be a true sacrifice for us, and one that may be asked of us. All these things will pass away like a flower that withers.

> We must avoid all complacency in the virtues we may have. To entertain any complacency would be vanity and perhaps amount to scorn of our neighbor. The Christian ought to esteem the virtues, not inasmuch as they are in him like

---

[32] *The Imitation of Christ*, Bk. III, ch. 31.

a personal possession, but inasmuch as they lead the soul to God.

When we receive consolations in prayer, we must not dwell on them with satisfaction; to do so would be to make of this means of drawing near to God an obstacle that would hinder us from reaching Him. It would be the equivalent of pausing in a selfish fashion over something created and making an end of the means. By so doing, we would set out on the road of spiritual pride and illusion. All that glitters is not gold; and we must be careful not to confound an imitation diamond with a real one. We should remind ourselves of our Savior's words: *Seek ye therefore first the kingdom of God and His justice; and all these things* (all that is useful to your soul and even to your body) *shall be added unto you* (Mt. vi. 33).

Therefore, we understand that adversity is good for us in order to deliver us from illusion and make us find the true road again.[33]

Suffering is like a wake-up call by which God tells us that this or that thing to which we are attached is in fact created, changeable, and passing away. Instead, in these times we must lift our hearts to Christ Crucified Who is uncreated, unchangeable, and will never pass away. In this way, we can thank God for sufferings because they give us this salutary occasion for detachment and union with Christ Crucified.

---

[33] Garrigou-Lagrange, *op. cit.*, 375-376.

Virtue Lies in the Mean

In our daily quest to embrace suffering for love of God, we must also remember that virtue is found in the moderation between excess and defect. Consequently, we must guard against an immoderate zeal by which a pious soul is often tricked by the devil into seeking out and embracing more suffering than lies in their capacity.[34] This leads to burn-out, exhaustion, and is really a fruit of pride and presumption.

Instead, St. Thomas observes that there is a virtue of "right recreation" (*eutrapelia*) which uses pleasures in a moderated way in order that the soul may rest and be rejuvenated (II-II q168 a2). This is necessary for pious souls and, hence, after the austerities of Lent the Church bids all men rejoice and feast for fifty days of Paschaltide. But here, too, we must be careful to not indulge to excess during our feasting at Easter, lest we squander whatever progress we might have made during Lent. Dom Scupoli, in praising the love of suffering, also discusses the need for rest:

> No one, however, is forbidden to exercise a proper prudence and diligence in providing for necessities, according to his position. For this is according to the Will of God, and is no impediment to peace or genuine spiritual progress. Let your purpose be in all things to do your duty according to your ability, and be indifferent and resigned as to all results, which are beyond you. There is one thing always in your power, and that is to offer to God your will, and desire no longer to will anything of yourself; for as soon as you have this freedom, and are detached on all sides (which you can be

---

[34] Cf. St. John Cassian, *Conferences* I, ch. 17.

always and everywhere, when occupied or not), you will enjoy tranquility and peace.[35]

In short, we must adhere to the will of God and understand that while we need suffering in order to achieve detachment, we also need rest to moderate our toil. St. Paul exemplifies this moderation and detachment when he says:

> I have learned, in whatsoever state I am, to be content therewith. I know both how to be brought low, and I know how to abound (everywhere and in all things I am instructed): both to be full and to be hungry: both to abound and to suffer need. I can do all things in him who strengtheneth me (Philip. iv. 11-13).

Here we may observe the fundamental lesson of humility: we need sufferings because we are attached to created things, and we need restful pleasures also since we are beginners in the spiritual life and cannot endure the great sufferings of the saints. Humility is conformity with the truth, and thus the pious soul uses these things properly in conformity with the truth (II-II q161). Thus, as the Apostle says, *in all things I am instructed.*

The Will of God

But even more than this, we see in the sufferings of Our Lord that we are instructed about the glory to come. In the Resurrection, we see that the true value of suffering is *conformity to the will of God*, which will overcome even death itself. It is the will of God that we venerate in the Cross. Whether we suffer or we rest from sufferings, we must conform to the will of God. And here we find hope for our

---

[35] Dom Lorenzo Scupoli, *Of Interior Peace or the Path to Paradise* contained within *The Spiritual Combat* (Scriptoria Books: 2012), 173, 174.

current crisis, wherein we must submit to the inscrutable Providence of God: *For if we live, we live unto the Lord; or if we die, we die unto the Lord. Therefore, whether we live or we die, we are the Lord's* (Rom. xiv. 8). Let us embrace the will of God, especially in sufferings, in order to be conformed to Jesus Christ and inherit eternal life.

> Learn, O my soul, in what manner thou shouldst accept whatever God sends thee. It may be a heavy Cross that he sends thee, but remember that it is imposed upon thee by God Himself. Thou wilt never be called upon to suffer as much as Jesus, and unless thou bearest thy Cross after Him, thou wilt never partake of His glory.[36]

---

[36] Fr. Ignatius, *op. cit.*, Day 20.

PART II
THE FIRST AND GREATEST COMMANDMENT

V

Public Enemy #1

In our time many Catholics spend a great deal of energy and stress worrying about things in the Church and in society that we cannot change. Ultimately there is a great deal that we simply cannot control.

There is one thing that we can control, however, and it really needs to be our first priority: our spiritual lives. We spend a great deal of time concerned about the enemies of Christ out there, but there is one enemy that should be our main concern before all others, because this enemy is not *out there*, but *right here*, even within you. And that is the subject of this chapter.

Growth in Charity

The aim of the spiritual life, and thus our whole lives, is growth in charity. This is quite literally *the meaning of life.* Garrigou-Lagrange writes:

> Christ incessantly reminds us that the supreme precept dominating all others and all the counsels is the precept of love[.]…Charity is the bond of perfection because it is the highest of the virtues which unites our soul to God. It ought to last forever, and it vivifies all the other virtues by rendering their acts meritorious,

ordaining them to the last end, that is, to its
object: God loved above all else.[37]

Thus the chief aim of all our spiritual practices must be the
growth in charity. If we spend our time in everything else but
this, our whole time will have been wasted. This why on the
Sunday before Ash Wednesday the Church proclaims these
sublime verses from the Apostle:

> If I speak with the tongues of men, and of
> angels, and have not charity, I am become as
> sounding brass, or a tinkling cymbal. And if I
> should have prophecy and should know all
> mysteries, and all knowledge, and if I should
> have all faith, so that I could remove
> mountains, and have not charity, I am nothing.
> And if I should distribute all my goods to feed
> the poor, and if I should deliver my body to be
> burned, and have not charity, it profiteth me
> nothing (I Cor. xiii. 1-3).

In other words, if you fast perfectly throughout Lent and
pray for hours, wearing a hair shirt, sitting in ashes all day
long, but do not grow in charity, you have wasted your time.
What is worse, you may have acquired the pride of demons
instead of the humility of saints. We must keep this aim in
mind for all our practices for Lent and throughout the year.

The Chief Enemy of Charity: The Predominant Fault

The supernatural virtue of charity (with the other virtues)
is given in holy baptism. Mortal Sin destroys charity in the
soul, but absolution restores charity with the other virtues. So
if we truly have these virtues, why are we not virtuous?
The virtues which are present within a soul in a state of
grace are blocked by the effects of Original Sin. Therefore, the

---

[37] Garrigou-Lagrange, *Three Ages of the Spiritual Life*, Vol. 1, 149, 150.

more the pious soul overcomes these effects by the power of grace, the more the virtues can show their effects. Above all, the predominant fault is the thing which prevents growth in charity and the other virtues. Garrigou-Lagrange defines it this way:

> The predominant fault is the defect in us that tends to prevail over the others, and thereby over our manner of feeling, judging, sympathizing, willing and acting. It is a defect that has in each of us an intimate relation to our individual temperament[.]... The predominant fault is so much the more dangerous as it often compromises our principle good point, which is a happy inclination of our nature that ought to develop and to be increased by grace[.]... In the citadel of our interior life, which is defended by the different virtues, the predominant fault is the weak spot, undefended by the theological and moral virtues. The enemy of souls seeks exactly this easily vulnerable point in each one, and he finds it without difficulty. Therefore, we must recognize it also.[38]

Thus in order to grow in charity, we must focus on our predominant fault. This is the weak point which is keeping us from advancing in the spiritual life. In Confession, we may feel overwhelmed with all of our sins and faults, and think that we need to focus on all our habitual sins at once. But this is a trick of the Devil, who seeks to turn you to despair if you do not advance on every front of the spiritual life at the same time.

Thankfully, we need not focus on every sin at the same time, but above all on our predominant fault. This is why the spiritual writers identify the predominant fault as one of the

---

[38] Ibid., 314-316.

three pillars of the spiritual life, together with prayer and spiritual reading. If we focus on this, our other sins will also be overcome. This is because it is the special fault to which we are particularly inclined by our natural temperament. As Garrigou-Lagrange continues, "a person's temperament must not be crushed; it must be transformed while keeping whatever is good in it."[39] Thus the first step in finding out your predominant fault is being aware of your individual temperament.

Temperaments

The spiritual writers follow the ancients in identifying four temperaments. A temperament is the manner in which God created you to be especially inclined. It is like your personality, but it can also be changed and other temperaments can be acquired by habit. The goal is to acquire the good qualities of all the temperaments while avoiding the defects of each.[40]

The temperament is the tied to the predominant fault because the Devil uses our natural temperaments to turn us away from our principle virtue and toward excess in sin:

> For example, a man is naturally inclined to gentleness; but if by reason of his predominant fault, which may be effeminacy, his gentleness degenerates into weakness, into excessive indulgence, he may even reach the complete loss of energy. Another, on the contrary, is naturally inclined to fortitude, but if he gives

[39] Ibid., 320.
[40] See Rev. Conrad Hock, *The Four Temperaments and the Spiritual Life* (1934). <http://www.catholicapologetics.info/catholicteaching/virtue/temperaments.htm>, accessed October 24, 2023. This book also includes a helpful self-examination to help find out your temperament.

free rein to his irascible temperament, fortitude
in him degenerates into unreasonable violence,
the cause of every type of disorder.[41]

Thus getting to know your temperament is a clue to
identifying your predominant fault. Here is a summary of the
four temperaments and their predominant faults according to
one priest:

> **Sanguine**: inflammable emotions—affable,
> energetic, enthusiastic, popular, expressive,
> insincere, noisy.
> *Predominant faults*: lust, gluttony,
> pusillanimity.
>
> **Choleric**: ardent emotions—daring, direct,
> decisive, insensitive, fearless, tactless.
> *Predominant faults*: anger, envy.
>
> **Melancholic**: deep emotions, disposition to
> sorrow—perfectionist, accurate, detailed,
> diplomatic, thoughtful, cautious, critical.
> *Predominant faults*: fear, aversion,
> despondency, despair.
>
> **Phlegmatic**: no strong emotions—kind, caring,
> gentle, soft-spoken, timid, relaxed, peaceful.
> *Predominant faults*: sloth, effeminacy.

To find out our predominant fault, Garrigou-Lagrange
adds fervent prayer to God to know our predominant fault,
observing our chief likes and dislikes ("Toward what do my
most ordinary occupations tend? What is generally the cause
of my sadness and joy?") as well as asking your spiritual

---

[41] Garrigou-Lagrange, *op. cit.*, 315. Here he is using the word
"effeminacy" in its traditional sense: a reluctance to suffer due to an
attachment to pleasure (II-II q138).

director. You may also ask your spouse or a trusted friend, who will often have a better knowledge of you than you yourself.

How to Overcome the Predominant Fault

Once we have identified our chief vice we must refocus all of our spiritual energy on combatting this one thing. This will be our key to the growth in charity. This begins with prayer. Offer your morning offerings for this purpose. Offer your rosaries for this aim. We are often enslaved to our chief passion because we are filled with pride. Let your prayer be humble and sincere. Choose a Psalm to say daily for this purpose: 3, 26 or 50, or one of the Seven Penitential Psalms.[42] Ask God for the grace to desire to suffer anything to overcome this.

Garrigou-Lagrange identifies two other aspects to this effort. The first is examination of conscience: "it is especially suitable for beginners to write down each week the number of times they have yielded to their predominant fault which seeks to reign in them like a despot."[43] The examination must be tied with frequent Confession, which not only absolves past sin but gives grace to avoid it in the future.

The other method given is called a sanction:

> It is also highly proper to impose a sanction, or penance, on ourselves each time we fall into this defect. This penance may take the form of a prayer, a moment of silence, an exterior or an interior mortification. It makes reparation for the fault and satisfaction for the penalty due it. At the same time we acquire more circumspection for the future. Thus many persons have cured themselves of the habit of cursing by imposing on themselves the

---

[42] See Appendix for a list of these Psalms.
[43] Ibid., 319.

obligation of giving an alms in reparation each time they fail.[44]

Imagine paying a dollar every time you commit this sin. Or skipping your next meal, or all seasoning at the next meal. This habituates your faculties to hate committing this vice, and turns your inclination away from it.

Do not waste your time or lose focus on this chief enemy that you may truly advance spiritually, and use the external practices for the necessary internal renovation. We spend all our energy on fixing things we cannot control, the Devil will laugh at us while we will fall back into sin.

---

[44] Ibid.

VI

Why Heretics Hate Mary
but We Should Love Her More and More

Marian devotion is the cure for heresy and the healing of all heretics. We must turn to her for refuge from the heretical depravity now consuming the Church. Marian devotion is the destruction of error, the fount of humility, and a potent safeguard for orthodox faith.

Mary Is the Destroyer of All Heresies

In *True Devotion to Mary*, St. Louis de Montfort writes:

> The most infallible and indubitable sign by which we may distinguish a heretic, a man of bad doctrine, a reprobate, from one of the predestinate, is that the heretic and the reprobate have nothing but contempt and indifference for our Blessed Lady, endeavoring by their words and examples to diminish the veneration and love of her. (30)

In the Tract for the Mass *Salve Sancta Parens*, the Church sings, "Rejoice, O Virgin Mary, thou alone hast destroyed all heresies." From this, Pope St. Pius X invoked her as "Destroyer of Heresies" in *Pascendi* 58. And again, it was in the context of St. Dominic's war against heresy that the Holy Rosary, Mary's psalter, was revealed.

Thus, it is manifest that Our Lady holds a special place in the relationship of Holy Church with heresy and heretics. Why is this? It is because the root cause of heresy is not anger, lust, or sloth, but pride. A formal heretic pridefully and obstinately rejects the authority of the Church and the authority of the Fathers. His whole opinion hinges on an imaginary antiquarianism created by his pride. And it is against the sin of pride that Our Lady most perfectly shows her power. This is why St. Louis says in another place:

> [Satan] fears her not only more than all Angels and men, but in some sense more than God Himself ...because Satan, being proud, suffers infinitely more from being beaten and punished by a little and humble handmaid of God, and her humility humbles him more than the Divine power (*True Devotion*, 52).

Demons and heretics fear her because she threatens to humble them. The latter impiously attack her under the pretense that they are safeguarding the honor due to God. In reality, they know that Mary will destroy their prideful opinions. *Humility is an abomination to the proud* (Ecclus. xiii. 24).

How Mary Humbles the Proud

When the Holy Spirit exalted Mary by the mouth of St. Elizabeth, Mary said:

> He hath shewed might in his arm: he hath scattered the proud in the conceit of their heart. He hath put down the mighty from their seat and hath exalted the humble (Lk. i. 51).

Devotion to Mary brings humility to the soul. Just as St. John heard her voice and leaped for joy, and St. Elizabeth immediately humbled herself, saying *Who am I that the mother of my Lord should come to me?* (Lk. i. 43), we too know this humility when we exalt Mary.

Mary humbles us because God wills that Jesus Christ be manifested to the world through her. According to nature, any man is her equal. According to grace and merit, she is "more honorable than the cherubim, and beyond compare more glorious than the Seraphim."[45] In Mary, our humility is truly tested because she is a human, not God.

Humility toward God is presumed by all, and heretics falsely think themselves humble because they say they submit to God. But their pride is revealed when they refuse to submit to man — both legitimate authority and the sayings of the wise. *The way of a fool is right in his own eyes: but he that is wise hearkeneth unto counsels* (Prov. xii. 15).

A humble man may even debase himself before wicked men, as Our Lord did. But heretics have no humility toward men. In reality, heretics are attempting to impose their private opinion on all authorities. They have no humility toward any human but are consumed in their own selves. As the history of Protestantism has shown, it is easy to feign humility toward God while exalting yourself over every man. This is the way of all the heretics.

One who is humble toward Mary will be humble toward authority. Mary especially checks the pride of heretics by proclaiming that they cannot have their own private, "personal Jesus," since Our Lord has forever bound Himself to His mother by His incarnation. In the same way that the Incarnation is the foundation of our redemption — without which there can be no Passion or Resurrection — the human person of Jesus Christ cannot exist without the person of Mary.[46] True union with Christ will result in love of Mary as our mother, who was also the first natural cause of His appearance to the world.

---

[45] Greek Catholic Marian antiphon.
[46] So too the mediation of the Sacraments — through another human — we receive our Lord.

Marian Devotion is a test for orthodoxy

Since Marian Devotion is the fount of humility, it becomes a powerful test for orthodoxy. For example, when St. John Vianney's lack of intelligence presented a barrier to his ordination, he was evaluated like this:

> The vicar-general asked the superior of the seminary: 'Is young Vianney pious? Is he devoted to the Blessed Virgin?' The authorities were able to assure him fully upon these points. 'Then,' said the vicar-general, 'I will receive him. Divine grace will do the rest.'[47]

And so the Church ordained the future patron of parish priests. Sometimes it is as simple as asking if a man has Marian devotion. If a man is truly devoted to Our Lady, he can be no heretic. St. Louis again:

> "If you follow her," says St. Bernard, "you cannot wander from the road." Fear not, therefore, that a true child of Mary can be deceived by the evil one, or fall into any formal heresy. There where the guidance of Mary is, neither the evil spirit with his illusions, nor the heretics with their subtleties, can ever come — *Ipsa tenente, non corruis* (*True Devotion*, 209).

Marian devotion is pleasing to God, because it shows Him that we are in desperate need not only of His help, but of human help as well. In this humility we are safe.

---

[47] Anonymous, *The Life of Saint John Vianney, The Cure of Ars* (Joseph Schaefer: New York, 1911), ch. 1.

VII

Conquer Effeminacy and Be a Man:
Five Things

In the next two chapters we will deal particularly with issues among Catholic men. This is because our forefathers responded to the crises of their times with true Catholic masculinity. This in turn helped and supported our foremothers who rose up as Catholic queens and noblewomen of home and society in dark times.

Why Effeminacy Must be Destroyed

St. Thomas defines effeminacy as a reluctance to suffer due to an attachment to pleasure (II-II q38 a1). Now it must be stressed that *effeminacy* as a vice is not the same thing as *femininity* as a perfection given by God to women. Femininity is good, whereas effeminacy is disordered—but this will not be treated here.

In men, effeminacy is especially abhorrent because it directly tears down the perfections of masculinity, which in particular are ordered toward the virtue of fortitude. As it is written, *Watch ye, stand fast in the faith, do manfully, and be strengthened. Let all your things be done in charity* (I Cor. xvi. 13). Thus it is especially important for men to root out and conquer effeminacy in order that they may be men of God. Since effeminacy is an attachment to pleasure and an avoidance of suffering, the man of God must reverse both of these to gradually develop a moderation toward pleasure and a desire for suffering. Here's how.

1. Cut out unnecessary Tech Pleasures

The harmful effects of technology must be taken seriously. In today's world, a man is flooded with targeted dopamine releases from every side. Music and movies, Facebook and Twitter, iPhones and iPads–all are designed by their makers to give you pleasure and make you attached.[48]

So the first step is easy: turn off all of these and start using only what is necessary. You need to call your wife? Fine, use your phone. You need to find an address? Fine, use the internet. But cutting off these pleasures will quickly remove a large portion of your attached pleasure and do it quickly, giving you a head start toward overcoming effeminacy. The goal is to become detached from the pleasure these things give so that even if you have to use them, you can say truly "I do not want this consolation."

St. John of the Cross says we should use this prayer any time we are forced by necessity to accept some created pleasure of any kind. This is because the man of God is detached from every created pleasure and adheres to Jesus Christ alone. St. Alphonsus:

> Whenever, therefore, any creature seeks to enter and to seize a portion of our heart, we must utterly refuse it admission; and then we ought to turn to Jesus Christ, and say to him: My Jesus, Thou alone art sufficient for me. I do not wish to love aught but Thee: *Thou art the God of my heart; and God is my portion forever* (*Means to Acquire the Love of God*, I).

We've already discussed this necessary detachment in a previous chapter. Here let us simply observe that although we

---

[48] The employees of these companies, for instance, do not allow their children to use these things. Nellie Bowles, "A Dark Consensus About Screens and Kids Begins to Emerge in Silicon Valley: 'I am convinced the devil lives in our phones,'" *New York Times* (Oct. 26, 2018).

must cut out all tech pleasures to work against effeminacy, it is sometimes necessary to use technology to fulfill the duties of your state in life. Technology can also be used for the virtue of *eutrapelia*, the virtue of games and right recreation. For example, a moderate use of technology for sports and entertainment is certainly legitimate for right recreation. But this can easily go to excess, since many of the programs built for screens are designed by their makers to cause an addiction, as we will discuss more below.

2. Cut off Unlawful Carnal Pleasure

The second and more strenuous battle is over carnal pleasure. Thankfully, cutting off technology will go a long way in this battle. Unfortunately, a man is still bombarded by immodesty every day unless he becomes a hermit. We will discuss this in more detail in the next chapter.

But one of the crucial aspects of this, of which we will speak again below, is changing your thinking about carnal pleasure. Every man has grown up with lies from TV and movies about carnal pleasure, and it is vital that he reverse his thinking and adhere to the truth. For example, the solitary sin, (especially with evil images) is perhaps the most effeminate thing a man can do (the Latin term *mollis* means "effeminacy," "softness/weakness," or "the solitary sin").[49] Why? Because chastity is the denial of pleasure (suffering), whereas the solitary sin is a reluctance to deprive yourself of pleasure because of your attachment to it. Thus the solitary sin perfectly manifests what effeminacy is.

Even worse, the society is so effeminate that it exalts the degradation of our sisters too, for the pleasure of effeminate men. Effeminate men actually think that it is masculine to seek

---

[49] The "solitary sin" is the traditionally modest phrase which refers to masturbation. "Evil images" here refers to pornography. Moral theologians have always employed these and other phrases for the sake of the virtue of modesty. I clarify them here to explain any misunderstanding.

carnal pleasure with a woman without marriage. They openly boast of this! Their attachment to carnal pleasure comes before the commitment (suffering) of Matrimony. How effeminate! As any converted sinner will tell you, the passing pleasure of the self-absorbed, carnal life is like night and day compared to a richly blessed life with wife and children all your life.

It is vital that you see these things truly as they are. The will follows the intellect (I q82 a3). How you think will determine how you act. It also turns your heart and your emotional life, as we will discuss below. When you begin to see the truth about effeminacy, you will eventually find these things utterly abhorrent because of their effeminate character, and love what is truly masculine: suffering for the love of Jesus Christ. That's why cutting out TV and movies will help here, since these images especially train our minds to believe errors about masculinity.

Instead, the most powerful remedy is undoubtedly the Holy Rosary. This prayer perfectly combines mental prayer and vocal prayer. Since so much of our bondage is in the images we have permitted into our memories, mental prayer is crucial to reverse this attachment and adhere rather to images of what is true: the life and virtues of Our Lord and Our Lady. Truly the powerful, salutary effects of this timeless devotion cannot be exhaustively praised.

If you are married, it is necessary to make the marital embrace not an occasion to satisfy your lusts, but to moderate also this pleasure like a man—for the sake of your spouse. Let her beauty first provoke in your heart a deep awe and *reverence* for her, and then a tenderness which seeks to make her feel safe and loved. Do not get caught up in the idea that she "owes you" this marital embrace, because this can quickly lead to effeminacy by creating a reluctance in you to suffer any absence of this embrace. Rather, work to sacrifice for her and put her needs before your own in this area and in all areas of your marriage continually. In this you are *taking care of your own body* (Eph v. 25)—who is your wife—so that you can truly die for her as a man of God (Eph. v. 25-31).

Only then will you be able to truly give your wife the Christian charity she deserves, and, by God's gift, raise up children for His Church.

3. Fast every week

Once you have renounced all unnecessary pleasure, you must work to acquire a love for suffering. From my view, the easiest way to start is to fast weekly. Effeminacy is an attachment to pleasure and fasting is detachment from pleasure. As such it is a crucial tool to use to overcome effeminacy.

Fasting must be loved by all men of God. This will be covered in a later chapter in more detail including practical tips for those just starting out.

4. Moderate your emotional life

This topic is also crucial to understand due to the widespread confusion. When we speak of emotions or "passions," we are referring to those movements of our concupiscible or irascible appetite that produce various emotions in our hearts (love, joy, desire, hatred, fear, anger, etc). Now these movements of themselves are not sinful, since sin is in the will. They can be, however, disordered and incline your will toward evil. Thus they are not entirely neutral.

In addition, other movements of our hearts are much more transcendent and spiritual – love, joy, peace. Or think of the feeling of a man's heart when he falls in love – this is not merely animal lust, but a deeply transcendent movement of his heart which calls forth a chivalric manhood. But these things too do not primarily come from acts of the will, but arise in our hearts by natural or supernatural causes. We might call these "affections," as opposed to the former, more base and animal-like "emotions."[50]

---

[50] For an introduction into the philosophy of the Heart in the spiritual life, see Dietrich von Hildebrand, *The Heart* (St. Augustine's Press, 2012).

But as men, we have a hard time regulating and moderating our affections and emotions. This can lead us to effeminacy if we are too consumed by our emotions and become attached to them, leading to a reluctance to suffer. On the other hand, it is common for men to attempt to be stoic and divorce themselves from all their affections and emotions, which leads to burn out or worse.

First, let's talk about emotions. We can make a distinction between antecedent and consequent emotions. The intellect knows the truth and moves the will to do the good. Then the emotions are ordered by the will toward the good. This is *consequent* emotion. The emotions are a consequence of the will ordering them toward the good. For example, during an arduous battle, the warrior who has the virtue of perseverance orders the irascible appetite toward the good and produces the passion of courage. Or again, the emotion of joy is produced when the intellect knows the true and the will rests in the good. The intellect thinking about the truth, which moves the will toward the good and the emotions to respond consequently and appropriately.

As a result of Original Sin, every man's will is weakened, his intellect is darkened, and his heart is inclined toward evil. This means that he has *antecedent* emotion. His emotions flare up and influence him *before* his intellect and will can do anything. Have you ever encountered something that made you so angry that you sinned with your tongue? This is an example of antecedent emotion. The passion of anger arose in your irascible appetite so vehemently that it moved your intellect and will to commit sin instead of the other way around. That is why it may actually be true when you say, "I'm sorry I did not know what I was saying. I did not mean it. I wasn't thinking." This common phrase reveals this truth: your intellect and will were moved by your emotions. It was a disordered, antecedent emotion that was not ruled by your intellect.

Consequent emotion, then, is truly masculine, whereas *antecedent* emotion inclines us toward effeminacy, particularly by our attachments in our concupiscible appetite, which seeks pleasure. However, we must further distinguish between *the perfect* and sinners like us. A truly ordered emotional life is only enjoyed by the perfect. To us sinners, we cannot avoid the burning of antecedent emotion even daily and it is foolish to think we can be perfect after only a short time of penance. Our fathers repented in dust and ashes for decades before they attained perfection. What pride for us to become discouraged if we fail even after a year in this!

By the action of grace, properly ordering your emotions toward the truth allows true affections to arise in your heart. This strengthens a man's heart to be the heart of a man of God. This is what is meant when the Holy Ghost says *Then did I run the way of thy commandments, when thou didst enlarge my heart* (Ps. cxviii. 32) and again, *Blessed is the man that feareth the Lord, his heart standeth fast and believeth in the Lord. His heart is established and will not shrink, until he see his desire upon his enemies* (Ps. cxii. 7-8).

A man should be focusing on meditating upon the Sacred Heart of Jesus or the Chaste Heart of Joseph. This is a very difficult but necessary part of being a man. And the first steps is being able to deal with your emotions so that your heart will be governed by the splendor of truth, not the chaotic waves of passions.

Therefore, we must take this knowledge about emotions and use it as a method of acquiring humility. When antecedent, disordered emotions arise, first cry to God and say: "O God, behold how disordered I am without Thy grace! Grant me the gift of self-knowledge." Then stop and think. This brings us to another helpful distinction: feelings and emotions. We may distinguish them like this:

Irrational passions = emotions
Passions + reason = feelings

Since our emotions are governed by our intellect, stopping to think breaks the cycle of overwhelming, antecedent emotion. All that is necessary is to stop, think, and ask yourself: "Why am I having this emotion?" Sometimes you may not get the answers quickly (or at all) but other times it becomes clear why an emotion is arising. Once the source is clear we can then distinguish between truth and falsehood.

Much of our antecedent emotional life is based on falsehood. In particular, the allurements of pleasures discussed above are all falsehoods. They promise happiness but never deliver. Since the intellect is ordered toward knowing the true, we must press our minds toward the truth. Because of our fallen state, we hate suffering, even though it is suffering that will help us to attain true happiness. When your emotions arise because of your reluctance to suffer, raise your mind to God and say:

> I thank Thee, Holy Father, that Thou hadst in love for Thy son disciplined me so that all my earthly affections may be stripped away and I may Thine and Thine alone.

Truly consider the fact that God in His charity has permitted some suffering to you so that you may be united to Him. This is the actual truth. When we meditate on the truth, our emotional life quiets down because it must submit to the truth by nature. Nothing can conquer a man who knows the truth and wills the good. Then his heart is strengthened.

On the other hand, sometimes emotions are based on truth, for example courage or joy as was mentioned above. These we may call "feelings," which can be used toward the good. When you think about your emotions and determine them to be based upon truth, you can then moderately will them (while avoiding any attachment) toward the good. For example, if we are inflamed with the passion of courage to overcome some difficulty and attain a good end, we can will this more and more to attain this end.

We can also use properly ordered feelings to excite the opposite passion in order to act against disordered passions and temptations. Scupoli observes, for example, that when we reject an evil thought (excepting lust), we can then bring it up and crush it again, strengthening a proper feeling toward it:

> First, whenever you are assaulted and buffeted by the impulses of the lower nature, you must resist them manfully, so that the higher will may not consent. Secondly, when the assaults have ceased, excite them again, so as to have an opportunity of overcoming them with greater force and energy. Then challenge them again a third time, so as to accustom yourself to repulse them with scorn and horror. These two [additional] challenges to battle should be made in the case of every unruly appetite, with the exception of temptations of the flesh (*Spiritual Combat*, ch. 13).

Notice what he says about "scorn" and "horror." These are those higher affections of the heart which respond to the truth about a thing, whether it is good or evil.

As I mentioned above, this moderation of our emotional life takes decades. Do not fall into prideful discouragement because you still struggle with your emotions. This process will take much time and energy but through God's divine grace you will overcome this aspect of effeminacy. A another aspect of this struggle in particular is man support, to which we now turn.

5. Get Man Support

One of the necessary steps for a boy to become a man is changing his support system from his mother to his father. The mother loves and nourishes the boy. The father loves and strengthens the man. Too many men today have had absent or effeminate fathers, and their mothers, because of the errors of feminism, have dominated the home. As a result a young man never truly grows into a man because this disordered home cannot properly help him through the transition from his mother to his father and thus become a man.

Ideally, a man has a strong father who is the head of the household, and the boy becomes a man through him. (Then a man takes the Virgin Mary as his mother and becomes the *protector* of his birth mother, not the other way around). Thus the first man support is your own father. But becoming a man means being initiated into *the brotherhood of men*. This is the second man support: to rely on strong masculine friendships to challenge you and strengthen you.

What is it about man support that is so important? God has given men the perfections necessary to build each other up into men. A woman is not given this perfection in the same way (she has other important gifts not treated here), and so a woman looks for her man to be *her man*, and is irritated and feels unsafe when she is forced to "mother" a man as if he were a boy. Men need support in their weaknesses, but this comes in a vital way from other men. When a man has the support of his brothers, he can then truly die for his wife like a man and care for her as she deserves.

Man support helps men sort out their emotions from their feelings. Talking to another man helps you see if your emotions are based on truth or falsehood.

Man support will challenge you to do all of the things above and naturally force you to be a man. This is all provided that you choose the right friends or have the fortune to have a strong father. A simple thing is to have one man who acts as your accountability, and talk with him once a week on the phone. Commit each new week to working on one aspect of manhood. Others have regular groups that meet and support each other.

Whatever works for your state in life, you must have man support for manhood. If you are deprived of good men all together, then read from the saints whose lives and writings are free online. Read the Holy Scripture and consider the men of God: Elias, Moses, Abraham, David, St. Paul, Our Lord

Himself. Choose a patron saint who can help you become a man–St. Joseph in particular, but also St. George, St. Thomas More, the Maccabean warriors and martyrs. You are not alone, brother. Fight the good fight, and God will give you the victory in time. Let us close by pondering the words of a great married saint, the man of God St. Thomas More. It is said he prayed these words while in prison before he gave his life in defense of the one true faith:

Give me the grace, Good Lord:
To set the world at naught.
To set the mind firmly on You and not to hang upon the words of men's mouths.
To be content to be solitary.
Not to long for worldly pleasures.
Little by little utterly to cast off the world and rid my mind of all its business.
Not to long to hear of earthly things, but that the hearing of worldly fancies may be displeasing to me.
Gladly to be thinking of God, piteously to call for His help.
To lean into the comfort of God.
Busily to labor to love Him.
To know my own vileness and wretchedness.
To humble myself under the mighty hand of God.
To bewail my sins and, for the purging of them, patiently to suffer adversity.
Gladly to bear my purgatory here.
To be joyful in tribulations.
To walk the narrow way that leads to life.
To have the last thing in remembrance.
To have ever before my eyes my death that is ever at hand.
To make death no stranger to me.
To foresee and consider the everlasting fire of Hell.
To pray for pardon before the judge comes.
To have continually in mind the passion that Christ suffered for me.
For His benefits unceasingly to give Him thanks.

To buy the time again that I have lost.
To abstain from vain conversations.
To shun foolish mirth and gladness.
To cut off unnecessary recreations.
Of worldly substance, friends, liberty, life and all, to set the loss at naught, for the winning of Christ.
To think my worst enemies my best friends, for the brethren of Joseph could never have done him so much good with their love and favor as they did him with their malice and hatred.
These minds are more to be desired of every man than all the treasures of all the princes and kings, Christian and heathen, were it gathered and laid together all in one heap. Amen.

VIII

Conquer Lust and Pornography:
Six Things

1. Always Flee

The Spiritual writers tell us that every deadly sin can be faced and conquered. For every deadly sin, we can cultivate the contrary virtue even while facing circumstances which provoke these sins. For example, to conquer anger, we can seek out that person that annoys us and intentionally speak kindly to them.

This holds true for every deadly sin *except lust*. This sin, because it comes from the generative power in man, as Scupoli writes, *must always been avoided at all costs*. There is never a time when a man should willfully put himself near any hint of temptation against purity. It is not conquered by facing it, but by flight. No man should ever presume himself strong enough to face this sin and survive. This holds for both a married man and a man who is not married. The lives of saints are replete with stories in which men took drastic action to avoid lust, or else perished. Scupoli writes:

> Do not presume on your own strength despite the fact that after many years spent in the world you have remained firm against the force of concupiscence. For lust often achieves in one instant what whole years could not effect. Sometimes it will make long preparations for the assault. Then the wound is more dangerous

when it comes least expected and under a disguise (*The Spiritual Combat*, ch. 19).

Therefore, immediately stop watching movies that have this suggestive content. Immediately turn away from all immodesty forced in front of you. Your spouse is the only one you should ever look upon–and even then, only with moderation. Always flee from this sin and be more willing to die than expose yourself to it. If you are forced by some necessity to be exposed, then keep your eyes down as much as possible and speak abruptly without forsaking charity. The spiritual writers are very clear on this: do not allow a false obligation to courtesy make you put down your guard with others.

2. Accountability and Frequent Confession

Once you have acknowledged that you are powerless against lust and must always flee, you have to get another man to be your accountability partner. This man's job is to keep you accountable to your good resolutions to conquer lust. He is someone to challenge you to fight manfully against this sin, and also someone to call upon when you are being tempted.

It is important to note that your accountability partner *should not be your woman*. Your woman needs to be able to rely on *you* to be the rock and confessing your sins to her (especially those of the flesh) only causes her grief and fear. Confess your falls to your brother, not your woman. Your brother will strengthen you, but your woman will be harmed by this.

Then you must frequent Confession. If you are falling into mortal sin, you must already be frequenting this Sacrament. Confession absolves your mortal sin, but also gives grace to overcome future sins. Even if you have no mortal sins to confess, you can piously confess venial sins as well, even though this is strictly not necessary in Confession (since venial sins are cleansed by Holy Communion). You can also mention past mortal sins against lust in order to increase in charity. However, confessing past mortal sins is not recommended for anyone with any temptation to scruples. However, this type of Confession (called a "Confession of devotion," or, if done less frequently, a "general Confession") is a great help for growing in holiness and overcoming lust.

3. Take refuge with the Blessed Virgin Mary

Our Lady is the Mother of Purity. Run to her when you flee of this temptation. Consider her Immaculate Heart and her Perpetual Virginity. She is your Mother. St. John Cassian says to think about your sister or mother when encountering this sin (*The Institutes*, Bk. VI). And who is more Immaculate or more our Mother than Our Lady?

When we run to Our Lady we feel ashamed of our weak nature in feeling the attraction to impurity. But instead of rejecting us, she helps us with the tenderness of a mother and gives us protection. If we have been unfortunate to fall into this sin, she keeps us from falling into despair and helps us return to the Lord.

Moreover, Our Lady is the most powerful human to obtain the grace of chastity to overcome this demon. What our own prayer cannot obtain, she obtains by her prayers. It shows the Lord humility when we ask Our Lady for help, because we acknowledge our unworthiness before Him. This humility fights against the pride of presumption when can cause a fall if you do not flee.

Finally, pray the Rosary. Mental prayer is essential for holiness but in particular this sin uses images to cause men to fall. The Holy Rosary is the easiest and most effective way to practice mental prayer. Take refuge in the mysteries of Our Lord and Our Lady and entrust yourself to her care.

4. Reject all scrupulosity

The Enemy wishes to make you fall, and then by scrupulosity to increase your pride and blindness and reliance on your self. Reject his machinations. If you fall, use the occasion for a greater humility and greater dependence upon God. Maintain your peace and run to Confession. For more on this, turn to the chapter on Scrupulosity.

5. Pray the violent Psalms

Most unfortunately, the reform of the Liturgy of the Hours removed much of the violent imagery from the Church's prayer book, the Holy Psalter. Our fathers used these verses to combat the very aggressive passions–especially lust–with a greater spiritual manliness. The passion of lust is, in one sense, the most powerful temptation because it is imbedded in our nature to procreate. Thus all unlawful desire must be cut off violently without a moment's hesitation, or else we quickly run the risk of consenting and falling into sin. Hear the words of the Doctor of Moral Theology:

> It is necessary to remark, that, when the thought which excites the delight is against chastity, we are, according to the common opinion of theologians, bound under pain of mortal sin to give a positive resistance to the delectation caused by the thought; because, if not resisted, the delight easily obtains the consent of the will. "Unless a person repel delectations," says St. Anselm, "the delight passes to consent, and kills the soul" (S. Ans. Simil., c. xl.). Hence, though a person should not consent to the sin, if he delight in the obscene object, and do not endeavor to resist the delectation, he is guilty of a mortal sin, by exposing himself to the

proximate danger of consent (St. Alphonsus, Sermon XVIII Sun. after Pentecost).

Therefore, let a man employ the weapons of prayer given by the Prophet:

In thy mercy thou wilt destroy my enemies. And thou wilt cut off all them that afflict my soul: for I am thy servant (Ps. cxlii. 12).

Let all my enemies be ashamed, and be very much troubled: let them be turned back, and be ashamed very speedily (Ps. vi. 11).

And I shall beat them as small as the dust before the wind; I shall bring them to nought, like the dirt in the streets (Ps. xvii. 43).
In the morning I put to death all the wicked of the land: that I might cut off all the workers of iniquity from the city of the Lord (Ps. c. 8).

6. Fast

We talked about this in the last chapter, but with this vice it is essential. For more on this, turn to the fasting chapter now.

Chastity is vital whether you are married or not, so let every man rise to the fight and conquer this demon which grips our world today. Victory is possible, as all our fathers attest. Do not lose hope and rise again and again to the battle until your enemy is crushed. *All nations compassed me about; and in the name of the Lord I will destroy them* (Ps. cxvii. 10).

IX

Don't Let Social Media Send you to Hell

The advent of the internet has opened wide possibilities to human communication, increasing man's ability to do great good and also great evil. I myself was converted to the Faith through contact with Catholics on the internet. This fact about the internet has helped spread the Gospel to souls who would be otherwise cut off from the message (we think here, in particular, of those under Muhammadan domination). It has also helped introduce more Catholics to beautiful liturgy that they may have never experienced otherwise.

Social media, however, was designed by its creators to psychologically manipulate its users into an addiction. As Facebook co-founder Sean Parker admits, they were "exploiting a vulnerability in human psychology... we understood this consciously and we did this anyway."[51] This was done through a system designed to effect every person on a fundamental level. Social media amplifies the natural response to human interaction, twisting it into a packaged, consumable unit of good feelings and mass-producing the effects a hundredfold. One sees the remarkable effects of this in any public place. The vast majority of people are sitting, standing, or walking around with their eyes fixed on a hand-held computer screen. Without a doubt, a man from the 1950s seeing this would think he had walked into a dystopian science fiction novel.

---

[51] "Facebook founder warns of social media addiction," *Good Morning America* (Nov 10, 2017) <https://www.youtube.com/watch?v=LPwR1i-sWpo>, accessed October 24, 2023.

Growth in Effeminacy

Social media works by giving consolations and then creating attachments to these consolations through "likes," "retweets," and "followers." This may seem unbelievable, but try paying attention to how you feel when you receive these throughout the day. Try putting your phone down for an entire day and see if you feel an urge to pick it up again to check for notifications. Most people feel an urge to pick up their phone and check within seconds of having any free time.

Attachments to these consolations leads to a growth in effeminacy. This is the foundation of social media's popularity and also its ability to be the cause of spiritual ruin. For the embracing of suffering is at the heart of the Gospel, as we discussed above.

But to one who is effeminate and attached to pleasures found in the world of social media, it becomes difficult to suffer with others. Social media takes away the normal face-to-face interaction we ordinarily have with our fellow man. Thus, it is easy to hurl insults at another person without saying it to their face, which would normally deter this sort of behavior. One can even do so anonymously online without any apparent consequence. But make no mistake, Our Lord clearly warns us that *every idle word that men shall speak, they shall render an account for it on the day of judgment* (Mt. xii. 36).

The Mortal Sin of Reviling

This brings us to the less obvious spiritual peril of social media. On the one hand, we are aware of the obvious spiritual peril of pornography and other such evils, but many Catholics may be surprised to read what St. Thomas says about reviling. This sin consists of publicly bringing dishonor to a person using words:

> Now railing or reviling deserves the punishment of hell, according to Matthew v.

22, *Whosoever shall say to his brother ... Thou fool, shall be in danger of hell fire.* Therefore, railing or reviling is a mortal sin.

... Since, then, railing or reviling essentially denotes a dishonoring, if the intention of the utterer is to dishonor the other man, this is properly and essentially to give utterance to railing or reviling: and this is a mortal sin no less than theft or robbery, since a man loves his honor no less than his possessions. If, on the other hand, a man says to another a railing or reviling word, yet with the intention, not of dishonoring him, but rather perhaps of correcting him or with some like purpose, he utters a railing or reviling not formally and essentially, but accidentally and materially.... Hence, this may be sometimes a venial sin, and sometimes without any sin at all.

Nevertheless, there is need of discretion in such matters, and one should use such words with moderation, because the railing might be so grave that being uttered inconsiderately it might dishonor the person against whom it is uttered. In such a case a man might commit a mortal sin, even though he did not intend to dishonor the other man: just as were a man incautiously to injure grievously another by striking him in fun, he would not be without blame (II-II q72 a2).

Here one may ask, *What does it mean to dishonor a man?* It is the opposite of honoring someone, which means to bear witness to the excellence of someone through signs or words (II-II, q. 103, a. 1). Thus, "honor" is a verb for manners and respect. Dishonor means to detract from the respect that someone deserves by virtue of who they are. St. James the Less expresses it this way in his New Testament Epistle:

> The tongue no man can tame, an unquiet evil, full of deadly poison. By it we bless God and the Father: and by it we curse men, who are made after the likeness of God. Out of the same mouth proceedeth blessing and cursing. My brethren, these things ought not so to be (Ja. iii. 8-10).

Man is made "after the likeness of God," and therefore he is deserving of honor and respect by his nature. St. Thomas points out that, with or without the intention of doing dishonor, reviling can be a mortal sin. Social media, through its constructed system of consolations and attachments, is able to facilitate a world of reviling without consequence but rather reward. St. Thomas says that "there is need of discretion in such matters, and one should use such words with moderation." But such things as these are not rewarded by the social media system, and there is always a temptation to revile another man in order to gain the virtual accolades of others. This has led many to enter into foolhardy disputes that would rarely occur in person, leading to spiritual and eternal peril.

Don't Be a Slave

Taking these things into consideration, it is essential that every soul learns to avoid slavery to social media in order to grow spiritually. Everyone needs to practice detachment from consolations, and that's why we have fasting and abstinence. Every earthly consolation needs to be moderated so that our spiritual lives may not be hindered, nor our souls fall into any kind of sin. This is true with phone notifications no less than with food. Therefore, it is fundamental to our spiritual lives to create space for detachments from pleasures such as Social media.

One method is to take one day per week, perhaps Sunday, to put your phone down and never pick it up for notifications until the following day. This may be hard at first, but this will only reveal how much you are attached to your phone. Another method is disciplining yourself to only look at your phone during certain times of the day.

Another consideration is this: Does this social media help me grow in my spiritual life? Am I more zealously fulfilling the duties of my state in life by using this app? If the answer to these is no, why not delete the app? If there is no profit to your soul, but rather detriment, then it is not worth it.

Furthermore, perform an examination of conscience: *Am I showing proper honor to others online, or do I fall into the sin of reviling? Can I tame my tongue or is it let loose by social media?* As we have seen, the saints have strong words for this vice, and it is not to be taken lightly. Even as secular and ecclesiastical politics continue to provide opportunities for disputes, we must hold fast to truth as well as to charity, so that we may not find ourselves in spiritual ruin.

If we can manage the negative effects of social media by God's grace, the technology can then be used for God's greater glory and the salvation of souls. This is the path that many saints have trodden before, as they used the new technology of their day to spread the Gospel and assist the Church. Let us be sons of our holy fathers, and, having purified ourselves from sin and attachments, let us take up this tool to use it for God's glory, and not our own. *Not to us, O Lord, not to us, but to Thy Name give glory* (Ps. cxiii. 9).

X

Fasting is a Foundational Virtue

Now that we've mentioned the importance of fasting in two chapters, it's time to dive deeper into this critically important aspect of our tradition.

Fasting: a Foundational Precept of Natural and Divine Law

Because of the dominance of lust and gluttony in fallen man in particular, the Fathers tell us that these two vices are the first vices to overcome in the spiritual life.[52] Therefore it is very difficult to make *any* advancement in the spiritual life if the concupiscible appetite is still dominated by these vices. Lust especially has a particular darkening effect on the intellect, as is shown with the total irrationality of our modern world.[53]

It may be readily seen how fasting curbs gluttony, but how does it help fight against the vice of lust? The reason is that they are both vices which affect the same concupiscible appetite. This appetite is what is naturally ordered toward two natural goods – food and the marital embrace: the two natural goods twisted by gluttony and lust. By fasting, the soul governs the appetite which is rebelling against right reason. Thus by fasting a soul attacks both vices with the same action.

---

[52] See John Cassian, *Institutes*, books 5 and 6.

[53] St. Thomas says that the vice of folly—the opposite of wisdom—comes as a direct result of the vice of lust (II-II q46 a3). For an excellent analysis of the effect of lust on folly in our modern epoch, see E. Michael Jones, *Degenerate Moderns* (Fidelity, 2012), who traces the relationship between the vice of lust and irrational folly in particular back to Luther, who broke his vows of chastity and promoted his errors to justify his sins.

Fasting, then, becomes the means by which the concupiscible appetite is moderated according to right reason. This turns the vice of gluttony into the virtue of temperance, and the vice of lust into the virtue of chastity. For this reason Augustine, summarizing the teaching of all the saints, says that "Fasting cleanses the soul, raises the mind, subjects one's flesh to the spirit, renders the heart contrite and humble, scatters the clouds of concupiscence, quenches the fire of lust, kindles the true light of chastity."[54]

St. Thomas adds: "everyone is bound by the natural dictate of reason to practice fasting as far as it is necessary for these purposes (II-II q147 a3)." The Natural Law itself indicates that fasting must be practiced, because a non-Catholic can see using his reason—as some do—that man is turned into a beast by his slavery to gluttony and lust.

Not only this, but God commanded the precept of fasting in the Old Covenant, establishing a severe penalty regarding the Day of Atonement as a fasting day: *Every soul that is not afflicted on this day [of fasting], shall perish from among his people* (Lev. xxiii. 29). At the time of Our Lord it was a common custom to fast on two days each week—Monday and Thursday—hence the mention of twice weekly fasting in the parable (Lk. xviii. 12). This practice was already established so that Our Lord gave no precept but simply said *When you fast, do not fast as the hypocrites* (Mt. vi. 16). Therefore the Christian tradition was established from Apostolic times to fast on different days than the "hypocrites" did, in order to distinguish the Christian from the Jew. A very early Church document is witness to this:

> [L]et not your fasts be with the hypocrites, for
> they fast on the second and fifth day of the

---

[54] *De orat. et Jejun.*, Serm. lxxii (ccxxx, de Tempore). Quoted in II-II q147, a1.

101

week; but fast on the fourth day and the Preparation.[55]

Thus Christians since Apostolic times have fasted each week on Wednesday—the day of Our Lord's betrayal—and Friday—the day of Our Lord's Passion. In the west a stronger focus was on the Passion of Our Lord, making Friday the primary day of fasting, although Wednesday and Saturday were also added during Embertide. Thus did the Apostles teach regular fasting, which developed into distinct customs in different regions.

Hence does St. Thomas say that fasting itself is a virtue, and therefore a habit which must be obtained by a regular practice—usually every week. St. Thomas, however, makes a further distinction with regard to the obligation to fast between the natural law of fasting and the divine law as mediated through the ecclesiastical authority. This means that the Church established the fasting rules according to the custom of every region, and he quotes Augustine as saying "Let each province keep to its own practice, and look upon the commands of the elders as though they were laws of the apostles."[56] Thus in the west and east different fasting rules obtained and were established according to the local custom, but all with the foundational obligation that fasting was necessary for the spiritual life.

Fasting as Penance and Contemplation

But besides the moderation of the concupiscible appetite, St. Thomas identifies two other ends of the virtue of fasting. The first is penance and satisfaction for sin, for which St. Thomas cites Joel II.12: *Be converted to Me with all your*

---

[55] The Preparation was the day before the Seventh Day. *Didache*, ch. 8. This is one of the earliest written records of the Apostolic teaching, written down circa 100 A.D.

[56] De Lib. Arb. iii, 18; cf. De Nat. et Grat. lxvii. Quoted in II-II q147 a8

heart, in fasting and in weeping and in mourning. Therefore it was particularly during the penitential season of Lent that the rules of fasting were enjoined by all Christian churches in every region (although with some particular differences in rules).[57]

But once moderation of the flesh and the penance were practiced, the third and highest end of fasting is shown:

> We have recourse to fasting in order that the mind may arise more freely to the contemplation of heavenly things: hence it is related of Daniel that he received a revelation_from God after fasting for three weeks.

Thus the fasting rules always enjoined not only flesh meats but also dairy products of milk and eggs. Why is this? The ancients could readily observe—even though their scientific terms were different—that these foods contained a great deal of fat which caused the bloating of the concupiscible appetite, leading to a sleepiness and dullness of the mind. Therefore fasting caused the appetite to be lightened with less food and less fat, and thus the intellect and heart could be more easily raised to contemplation.

This is the reason that fish was the only meat allowed, due to it being a lean meat with little fat. This also explains the origin of Shrove or Fat Tuesday (or Carnival meaning "goodbye to meat"), the day on which all the eggs and milk were meant to be used up—with various customary delights such as the Polish Pączki—as they were not eaten again until Easter. And thus does St. Thomas summarize this importance

---

[57] The custom of eating fish during Lent never obtained in the east for example, which abstained not only from fish but from wine and olive oil. This is probably an indication of the economic differences between the rural western Provinces (especially to the north) and the many urban centers that dominated the eastern provinces.

of fasting for the devout contemplation on feast days throughout the year:

> At the Easter festival the mind of man ought to be devoutly raised to the glory of eternity, which Christ restored by rising from the dead, and so the Church ordered a fast to be observed immediately before the Paschal feast; and for the same reason, on the eve of the chief festivals, because it is then that one ought to make ready to keep the coming feast devoutly. Again it is the custom in the Church for Holy orders to be conferred every quarter of the year [at Embertide]... and then both the ordainer, and the candidates for ordination, and even the whole people, for whose good they are ordained, need to fast in order to make themselves ready for the ordination.

Thus did our fathers fast and abstain in this long established custom of fasting in every region of the Church. But it was not only the foundational precept to overcome the basic vices of lust and gluttony, but a regular discipline of rigor by which the saints ascended the heights of contemplation and offered to God reparations for the sins of men.

Modern Errors Concerning Fasting

In modern times a suppression of fasting has been justified with a twofold error: one in the doctrine and spiritual life, the other in an erroneous assertion about the state of the modern world. This is the irrational and temerarious assertion that Modern Man had progressed beyond the need for rules for things such as fasting, and can control his own appetites.

But in doctrine, it was asserted (or at least implied) that works of charity can replace the mortification of fasting

without any loss to the spiritual life.[58] But works of charity—
although good and laudable in themselves—do not check the
excess of the concupiscible appetite. The spiritual life is
hindered because the foundational vices are not attacked at
their root.

Then a neo-Gnosticism prevailed, asserting that
mortification was solely interior and need not concern the
body. But this error was worse than the first, since it denied
the basic constitution of man as both soul and body integrated
into one person.

But this fed into the most egregious error of all, which said
that man was suited more for liberty than law. This was
nothing but a rhetorical cloak by which Fallen Man could hide
forever the shame of his Original Sin. The denial of this
dogma—at least in practice—lies at the heart of this twisted
abuse of liberty against law, in order given the sins of the flesh
full license and no restraint, leading to a complete slavery to
sin and spiritual blindness. Such is the state of the modern
world in our day, due in large part to the surrender of the
Catholic shepherds and faithful to the raucous demands of
enslaved Fallen Man.

How To Fast: Practical Wisdom from The Fathers

Given all this, it is crucial that Catholics who wish to
advance in the spiritual life reclaim once again the discipline
of our fathers in the virtue of fasting. There is no better time to
regain this than in the Great Fast of Lent, but one can start the
weekly fast at any time of the year, as we have already said.

Once a soul has been convinced of the need for fasting, it
is crucial to avoid the most common error identified by the
Fathers in this matter: immoderate zeal.[59] The Devil takes the
pious intentions of a generous soul, and twists them to think
that if they do not take on a rigorous discipline of full
abstinence and daily fasting, they are not truly fasting. As a

---

[58] Paul VI (1966), *Paenitemini*
[59] John Cassian, *Conferences* I, ch. 17

result these souls burn out and fail after two days and fall into despondency, and stop fasting all together.

Instead, have humility to look at yourself as objectively as possible: what amount of fasting can you do in order to gain a habit of fasting? Start by abstaining from meat on all Fridays (not just in Lent). Once you can do that with regularity, start skipping breakfast on Friday. Once this has become a habit, consider making it a full fasting day by eating only one meal on Friday. In Lent, you can do the same for Wednesdays as well. If you do this you are on your way to the virtue of fasting. Our fathers took only one meal six days a week in Lent and abstained from meat and dairy even on Sundays.

Be careful during Paschaltide: it is easy to lose your whole virtue of fasting by giving into an excess of feasting during this feast of feasts. It is proper to relax all fasting during this time, but it is also wise to not completely remove fasting. Continue, for example, some abstinence on Fridays during Paschaltide, then regain the full fasting discipline during the time after Pentecost.

It is also very helpful to do this with other faithful (as it was once practiced in Lent). Consider fasting with your spouse or joining an Exodus 90 group, or the Fellowship of St. Anthony or St. Nicholas. By maintaining this regular fasting discipline you will, by God's grace, have the fundamental weapon in place to combat the demon of lust and gluttony, and achieve holiness.

XI

Against the Vice of Curiosity

St. Thomas defines the vice of curiosity as "when a man is withdrawn by a less profitable study from a study that is an obligation incumbent on him" (II-II q167 a1). I've heard another priest define it as "Inordinate desire for useless or profane knowledge." The opposite vice is negligence, defined as "lack of due solicitude" (II-II q54 a1) elaborated by Prümmer as "the voluntary omission of knowledge essential to one's state and condition of life (no. 527)." So we have curiosity which is an excessive desire for knowledge, and negligence, which is *not enough* desire for knowledge.

The virtue and mean is studiousness, which is "the virtue in which one pursues knowledge according to one's state in life."[60] Each state of life has duties and those duties require knowledge. The first duty of every state is to know the Faith essentials for your salvation and then those practical matters particular to your state.

As any parent has the duty to protect their children, they must take care to have some knowledge about the world of politics both secular and ecclesiastical. This helps us to develop the virtue of caution in this crisis (to see and avoid future evil), which is necessary to protect our children. However, it is not incumbent upon any parent to delve completely into the endless research of these doubtful matters, since it creates a danger of curiosity, in which a parent will forsake the duties of their state in life. Therefore, let the reader beware of curiosity and not be taken by *fables and endless genealogies, which furnish questions rather than the*

---

[60] Ibid.

edification of God which is in faith (I Tim. i. 4). Or again the Holy Ghost declares:

> Seek not the things that are too high for thee, and search not into things above thy ability: but the things that God hath commanded thee, think on them always, and in many of his works be not curious. For it is not necessary for thee to see with thy eyes those things that are hid. In unnecessary matters be not over curious, and in many of his works thou shalt not be inquisitive. For many things are shewn to thee above the understanding of men. And the suspicion of them hath deceived many, and hath detained their minds in vanity (Ecclus. iii. 22ff).

Knowledge of the history and nature of the crisis can be good for the faithful to properly respond, but we must also realize that much of this evil will remain hidden from us and known only to God. Take what is helpful to know for the duties of your state, and leave the rest to God.

The Necessity of Keeping your Peace Undisturbed

But even if we avoiding unnecessary knowledge, it is easy to be disturbed. We might become agitated, anxious, or wrathful. We can be tempted to pusillanimity—which is failure to do what lies in your power (II-II q133 a1)—or despair, which is conforming your emotions to a denial of God's goodness and power (II-II q20, a1, 3). Both of these vices are related to sloth and effeminacy. Hence a man must first understand that these disordered emotions lead him to vice and sin and are thus tools of the Devil to destroy his soul. Then he must fight against them manfully.

Now peace is defined by St. Thomas as the "tranquility of order" in which "all the appetitive (emotional) movements in one man are set at rest together" (II-II q29 a1). And whereas

WHEN THE GATES OF HELL PREVAIL

the former vices are a result of sloth, peace is the result of charity which is union with God (Ibid., a3). When we advance in charity to God, our emotional life is quieted because our soul is properly ordered, with reason and will governing our emotional life so that it is properly expressed. Then our hearts contemplate truth with spiritual affections. Thus, for example, our reason guides us to become angry when anger is proper, but it also moderates the pleasures of wrath by meekness, so that we seek a just vindication, not an excess of cruelty (II-II q158 a1). And if we have a virtuous anger, it is with utter tranquility of heart and peace of mind. Since your peace is proportionate to your charity, any lack of peace is evidence of a lack of charity and holiness. So pick up your cross.

Keeping your Peace

Dom Scupoli states that "The whole and principle business of your life must consist in continually quieting your heart, and never letting it go astray."[61] For truly when a heart is perfected in charity, there is nothing which can disquiet it because it is united to the One Uncreated and Unmoved. As it is written, *Thou wilt keep him in perfect peace, whose mind is stayed on thee* (Is. xxvi. 3) and again

> Our God is our refuge and strength. Therefore we will not fear, when the earth shall be troubled; and the mountains shall be removed into the heart of the sea (Ps. xlv. 2-3).

All the spiritual writers say that the way in which we must obtain this peace is through rejecting every created consolation—even spiritual consolation—and clinging to God alone. Thus we embrace suffering because it blesses us with the detachment needed to achieve inner peace. Scupoli:

---

[61] Lorenzo Scupoli, *Of Interior Peace or the Path to Paradise* contained within *The Spiritual Combat* (Scriptoria Books: 2012), 163.

> You must toil and make every effort, especially at the beginning, to embrace tribulation and adversity as your dear sisters—desiring to be despised by all, and to have no one who entertains a favorable opinion of you, or brings you comfort, but your God.[62]

You must continually embrace suffering until you come to a place where you actually desire it because you know what great help it is to charity and union with God.

It is thus that we must approach this crisis in the Church—with a great desire to suffer. Let a man examine himself and see whether his peace is disturbed by reading the news or investigating controversy. If he is disturbed, let him drop everything and come back to the Lord, fighting strenuously against the temptations toward effeminacy and embracing the cross. It is unwise to enter battle before one is properly prepared to fight and overcome. Therefore attend to your soul, lest it be lost on the Day of Judgment. Abide in charity with God and acquire peace and detachment before you engage with these lesser matters.

---

[62] Ibid., 165.

XII

When Scruples are Pride Disguised as Virtue

Prümmer defines scrupulosity as "a state of groundless fear rather than the judgment of a sound mind" (no. 144). He identifies the signs of scruples: an excessive anxiety about previous Confessions, protracted accusations of irrelevant details, stubbornness that refuses to accept the decisions of the confessor. Scruples affect a soul devoted to God and sensitive to offending Him. Take heart, brother: many saints have struggled as you do.

But know the truth: scrupulosity is the trick of the Devil, who takes your sin and casts fear into your heart. He says you are unforgivable, or that you are such a sinner that you are beyond God's mercy. Thus, it is often tied with the sin of despair, which is a sin against hope. He even causes you to feel a pleasure, causing you to think this is virtuous. But if this is the source of your scruples, this is pride. (We will deal with other forms of Scruples in the next chapter.)

Why is it pride? Because the tribunal of God says, "I absolve you from your sins." But you refuse the tribunal of God. You are imagining a tribunal that is higher than God. Who are you to judge God's own judgment of you? *Be you humbled under the mighty hand of God* (I Pet. v. 6) — both in His punishments and His mercies. Do not pridefully exalt yourself above Almighty God. You are not above or beyond God's mercy, for God's mercy has been applied to you. Our Lord Jesus shed His Precious Blood to merit for you this mercy. Do not scorn His sufferings on the pretense that you are unworthy. Yes, you are unworthy. But God has made you worthy by the Blood of Jesus Christ.

Scrupulosity Is Trusting in Self and Not in God

If the foundation of the spiritual life is distrust of self and trust in God, scrupulosity uses pride to reverse this. It pridefully refuses God's mercy and causes a soul to trust more in its own thoughts and deliberations than in the power and mercy of God. Besides the pride regarding Confession, scrupulosity also manifests itself in a paralyzing anxiety about sin. Scruples causes a man to agonize over the question: did I sin? Was this a sin? Am I sinning?

Stop trusting in yourself. Get out of your head. You are trusting in yourself to know the answer. Instead, follow these steps strictly and shun every other anxiety:

1. Ask the Holy Spirit to enlighten you with this prayer: *Come Holy Spirit, enlighten my mind, that I may know the sins that I have committed either by thought, word or deed, and give me the grace of true contrition.*
2. Think as objectively as possible: did I sin? If necessary, ask a trusted friend. A good, objective guide is Prümmer. Do not take more than five minutes on this. Set a timer if you need to.
3. Now be silent before God and truly listen. Do not take more than two minutes on this. God will show you the sin, or He will be silent.
4. If you have sinned, immediately use this as an occasion for humility (see below). If He is silent, trust in Him.[63]

This method is based on trusting in God's mercy. God *will have all men to be saved, and to come to the knowledge of the truth* (I Tim. ii. 4), and again, *every one that shall call upon the name of the Lord shall be saved* (Joel ii. 32). Trust in these promises from God. If He is silent, trust that you have not sinned, and continue as before. If you have sinned, He will show you, because He desires your salvation.

---

[63] These practical tips were shared with me by a wise confessor and have helped me.

Use Every Fall for Humility, Not Pride

If you have fallen into sin, the demons will rush at you to cast fear and anxiety into your heart. Instead of succumbing to their pride and despair, humble yourself. Recognize your utter dependence upon God's grace to overcome this, and pray, in the words of Scupoli:

> When you realize that you have been wounded by sin, whether through weakness or malice, do not lose your courage or become panic-stricken. Turn to God with a great and humble confidence saying: "See, O Master, what I am able to do. When I rely on my own strength, I commit nothing but sins."
>
> Meditating on this, recognize the extent of your humiliation and express to our Lord your sorrow for the offense committed. With an unperturbed heart, indict your vicious passions, especially the one that has occasioned your fall, and confess: "O Lord, I would not have stopped at this had not Your goodness restrained me."
>
> Give thanks to God, and more than ever give to Him the complete love of your heart. What generosity on His part! You have offended Him, and, despite this, He extends His hand to prevent another fall (*Spiritual Combat*, ch. 26).

Your sin was caused by trusting in yourself. Turn your trust away from yourself, therefore, and trust in God. *You must thank God that He has prevented a greater fall.* Maintain your peace, and run to confession.

Despair is a Sin against Hope

We mentioned before how despair as a sin against hope, which is "conforming our mind to a false opinion about God" (II-II q10 a1). Therefore, you must ask God to strengthen the virtue of hope within you. Shun despair by praying the Act of Hope until you believe these words through and through: "O God, relying on Thy almighty promises and the infinite merits of Christ, I hope to obtain remission of my sins and everlasting happiness with Thee. In this hope I intend to live and die."

Fear and anxiety are from the demons. Peace is from union with God.

It vital to understand that God does not cast paralyzing fear or anxiety into your heart. This is the work of demons. This fear causes you to focus on yourself and trust in your own wisdom. True fear of Lord is the beginning of true wisdom because it brings forth humility. Humility causes a man to focus on God and distrust Himself. Therefore, reject all paralyzing fear and anxiety as from the demons. Utilize sacramentals and trust in God's power and not your own. Realize that anxiety is evidence of attachment to creatures, and renounce all attachments and love suffering. Know that peace is the fruit of charity, which is union with God (II-II q29 a3). Strive with all your energy to maintain your peace, because this means maintaining your union with God. Peace will come after much suffering. *Cast thy care upon the Lord, and he shall sustain thee: he shall not suffer the just to waver for ever* (Ps. liv. 23).

XIII

Untangling the Stages of Sin

Let us consider the seven stages of sin broken down this way:

1. Suggestion
2. Pleasure
3. Consent
4. Act
5. Habit
6. Slavery
7. Spiritual Blindness

In this chapter we're going to focus only on the first three steps which help to understand the heal scruples. The first step, suggestion, bears upon the distinction between Original Sin and actual sin. Original Sin is a condition, not a moral action. It refers to a darkened intellect, a weakened will, and a heart inclination to evil. In order to be healed from this wound, all men need the grace of God through Our Lord Jesus. But the crucial point to seize upon here is that a suggestion to sin, stemming from our fallen condition, is not an "actual sin." In other words, there is no need to go to Confession for suggestions to sin. By contrast, as the Baltimore Catechism says: "Actual sin is any willful thought, word, deed, or omission contrary to the law of God" (Question 52).

The crucial difference is in an *action of the will*. Suggestions to sin are not actions of a man's will, but happen to him without involvement of his will. We will return to how the will is involved below.

What is the nature of these suggestions? Suggestions are thoughts, emotions, and inclinations that are internal. These are known as *logismoi* among the Greek Fathers. There are three places they come from: the world, the flesh, and the devil. In our flesh, wounded by Original Sin or psychological factors like Obsessive Compulsive Disorder, we can feel an overwhelming inclination toward scruples.

Healing from Evil Thoughts

There are many factors that can help heal a soul from evil thoughts. One aspect is what we put into our imagination. Evil suggestions can be mitigated by daily prayer practices that use the imagination – the Rosary or mental prayer – and restricting all evil images (contained in movies) as much as possible. This helps keep your imagination focused on the things of God and helps to heal this faculty of the pollution of the world, the flesh, and the devil. Especially if you are a man struggling with a severe psychological condition, this healing may take years. But persevere, brother, for Our Lord has given His infallible promise: *Come to me, all you that labor, and are burdened, and I will refresh you* (Mt. xi. 28).

Another crucial point here is that emotions can also be suggestions to sin. For example, a sudden flare of anger may arise in you and be overwhelming. But still, if your will has not yet acted, you have not sinned. You must learn over time to moderate your emotional life. Emotions arise from our sensual appetites, and Original Sin causes our sensual appetites to overwhelm our souls. As we grow in virtue, we must learn to govern our emotional life with our intellect and will. Again, this takes time. Additionally, on the level of sensual appetites, it is crucial to fast as we have already discussed.

But most of all, frequent reception of Holy Communion is essential. In this great Sacrament, our venial sins are cleansed. In this we also place our trust in the Lord's power and not our own. Overcoming these difficulties requires the cessation of trusting in ourselves and turning all of our trust to God. On the level of suggestions to sin, we must have the humility to see ourselves as disordered but to trust that God is infinitely greater than our worst evil. By ourselves we are sinners, yet with God we can become holy.

Willful Pleasure

We next move to the second stage of sin, and this is where the distinctions become difficult. This is because under Original Sin, it is difficult to distinguish in our minds when we examine our conscience. This is why, especially with scruples, we must trust in God and not primarily our own intellect when examining our conscience.

Pleasure is something more complex, because we may say pleasure can be found in different faculties and powers of the human soul and body. On the one hand, there is a certain pleasure intellectually, as when a man sees a beautiful array of stars and marvels. This intellectual pleasure is an immediate apprehension by the intellect of beauty and does not involve the will.

There is also a sensual inclination to pleasure, such as when a man who is hungry sees and smells a delicious plate of his favorite food. His concupiscible appetite is immediately inclined to this pleasure. Still, his will has not yet acted.

In these two examples, we introduce suggestions into our intellect that are not necessarily suggestions to sin. As I emphasized above, even evil suggestions are not actual sins. What makes a sin a sin is always an action of the will. Prümmer, following St. Thomas, defines a willful act as "that which proceeds from an internal source of action accompanied by knowledge of the end sought" (no. 20).

So we first have the intellectual pleasure we mentioned, as well as the sensual pleasure inclination. What happens next is that your will makes a choice. You may choose to turn toward the pleasure or turn away. In other words, by our will, we may choose to *continue* to have this pleasure or not. It is the reaction of your will which counts. If the pleasure is in something good, then the choice to continue it is also good.

But if that pleasure is in any way evil, then taking pleasure is also evil. As St. Thomas observes, "pleasure in a good action is good and in an evil action, evil" (ST Suppl. q49 a6).

Summing up what we have said so far, the Doctor of Moral Theology explains it this way:

> The suggestion is the first bad thought that is presented to the mind: this is no sin, but, when rejected is an occasion of merit. "As often," says St. Antonine, "as you resist, you are crowned." The delectation [willful pleasure] takes place when the person stops, as it were, to look at the bad thought, which by its pleasing appearance, causes delight. Unless the will consents to it, this delectation is not a mortal sin; but it is a venial sin, and, if not resisted, the soul is in danger of consenting to it: but, when this danger is not proximate, the sin is only venial (St. Alphonsus, *Sunday Sermons*, Sermon XLVII).

Thus, the action of the will enters in at the pleasure stage of sin. Here is where we may commit a venial sin by "entertaining" an evil thought: choosing to continue to have pleasure in something sinful. We must note here that St. Alphonsus also states that if this pleasure is against purity, it is not venial, but mortal, since these pleasures lead immediately to consent by a proximate danger.

Consent

If a willful act includes an action of the will and knowledge of the thing sought, Prümmer then makes the following distinction: "if the knowledge is intellectual the voluntary act is perfect; if it is sense-knowledge the voluntary act is imperfect" (no. 20). By this we may distinguish between willful pleasure and willful consent. In the former, a soul simply chooses to have more sensual pleasure — normally venial, unless it is against purity. In the latter, he moves his intellect to intentionally pursue this pleasure — this may cause a mortal sin, depending on the gravity of the thing sought. That is why consent is the final internal stage of sin, which immediately leads to the first external stage: act. This seems to be why Our Lord connects the internal sin of adultery with the external, and the internal sin of murder with the external (Mt. v. 21).

In a man's labors under scruples and Original Sin, it is crucial that a soul seek and find a knowledgeable confessor in order to untangle these distinctions to bring clarity and peace to his mind. If no good confessor can be found, seek the support of a spiritually mature and charitable friend. Read the spiritual classics, and practice mental prayer. When tempted to despair, pray the Act of Hope continually. Persevere in prayer, and God will grant you rest from your enemies in due time.

> Who can understand sins? from my secret ones cleanse me, O Lord:
>
> And from those of others spare thy servant. If they shall have no dominion over me, then shall I be without spot: and I shall be cleansed from the greatest sin.
>
> And the words of my mouth shall be such as may please: and the meditation of my heart always in thy sight. O Lord, my helper, and my redeemer. (Ps. 18:13–15)

XIV

Gratitude:
The Safeguard of Humility

One of the two soldiers who had to lead him
caused him all possible sufferings. He was
forced to make long marches, was exposed to
the rays of the sun, to the rains and the cold of
the nights. His body, already weakened by
several severe illnesses, finally broke down[.]
… In the morning Chrysostom had asked to rest
there on the account of his state of health. In
vain; he was forced to continue his march. Very
soon he felt so weak that they had to return to
Comana. Some hours later Chrysostom died.
His last words were: *Doxa to Theo panton
eneken* (Glory be to God for all things).[64]

Humility means conformity with the truth (II-II q161). The
truth is that every good comes from God. *None is good but
one, that is God* (Mk. x. 18), and *every perfect gift is from
above, coming down from the Father of lights* (Ja. i. 17).
Therefore, a life of thanksgiving to God is in conformity with
the truth. The proud rebel against the truth and thus live a life
destitute of gratitude. Unhappy sinners, they are consumed in
lies as their minds are darkened by transgressing the truth. The
just man who knows the truth will give glory to God for all
things.

---

[64] C. Baur, "St. John Chrysostom," *Catholic Encyclopedia* (1910).

Existence

The first gift of God is existence itself. *Thy hands have made me and formed me* (Ps. cxviii. 73). What did you do, O Man, before you existed to deserve your existence? Before you existed, you were nothing. Bergamo observes:

> God has shown His creative omnipotence by forming me out of nothing and making me a human being. Were God to withdraw his omnipotent preserving hand from me I should at once show what I am capable of when left to myself, by returning immediately into nothingness.[65]

We say in the creed, *I believe in God the Father Almighty, Maker of Heaven and Earth.* Not only are you created by God, but your very existence at this moment is preserved by Him. Were He to withdraw His will for your existence at this moment, you would cease to be. God brought you into being on account of His great mercy and preserves your existence now according to His mercy. Give thanks to God for your creation.

Election to Grace

Our creation in the natural order is a mercy from on high. Our recreation in the supernatural order is a grace from the Hand of God.

> If anyone affirms that we can form any right opinion or make any right choice which relates to the salvation of eternal life, as is expedient for us, or that we can be saved, that is, assent to the preaching of the gospel through our natural

---

[65] Bergamo, *Humility of Heart* (TAN reprint, 2018), 14.

powers without the illumination and inspiration of the Holy Spirit, who makes all men gladly assent to and believe in the truth, he is led astray by a heretical spirit, and does not understand the voice of God who says in the Gospel, *For without me you can do nothing* (Jn. xv. 5), and the word of the Apostle, *Not that we are competent of ourselves to claim anything as coming from us; our competence is from God* (II Cor. iii. 5).[66]

You have the true faith. You are in the state of grace. You are a Catholic. But this is not because of you and your merits, but the grace of Almighty God Who shows mercy to sinners. Do not take pleasure in seeing the ignorance of poor sinners while you have the truth, for the truth is a gift from God.

Did you receive holy baptism while still an infant? Then what did you do to deserve it? Did you receive holy baptism after a life of sin? Then what did you do to deserve it? It was the priest who said over you: "Depart from him, unclean spirit, and give place to the Holy Spirit, the Advocate."[67]

He has *delivered us from the power of darkness, and hath translated us into the kingdom of the Son of his love* (Col. i. 13). In the beginning *darkness was upon the face of the deep* (Gen. i. 2) just as you were nothingness before God called your soul into existence. So too in the *laver of regeneration* (Tit. iii. 5) God has said to a dead man, *Lazarus, come forth* (Jn. xi. 43) and to a sinner, *Zacchaeus, come down* (Lk. xix. 5). What did you do to deserve your calling to eternal life? As David says, *Who am I, O Lord God, and what is my house, that thou hast brought me thus far?* (II Kings vii. 18). Give thanks to God for your election to grace.

---

[66] Synod of Orange (529), Canon 7.
[67] Rite of Baptism, At the Door of the Church.

Good Works

If you have been called forth out of nothing, and called to eternal life and been converted to the truth, you must have faith and works in order to be saved. As it is written, *in Christ Jesus neither circumcision availeth any thing, nor uncircumcision: but faith that worketh by charity* (Gal. v. 6). Have you overcome sin? Have you advanced in virtue? Have you shown mercy to the poor?

If you have done any good work, this is the work of God. *Not to us, O Lord, not to us; but to thy name give glory* (Ps. cxiii. 9). This is the reason for the rule of the saints: "To refer what good one sees in himself, not to self, but to God. But as to any evil in himself, let him be convinced that it is his own and charge it to himself."[68]

It is false humility to deny your virtue. If it is true that you have virtue, have the humility to admit it. But do not exalt yourself as the proud man and say, *I give thee thanks that I am not as the rest of men, extortioners, unjust, adulterers, as also is this publican* (Lk. xviii. 11), for this thanksgiving is abhorrent to the Almighty. But give thanks, rather, to the One who has worked this good in you. For it is *God who worketh in you, both to will and to accomplish, according to his good will* (Phil. ii. 13). Or as the Doctor of Grace proclaims: "Your good merits are God's gifts, God does not crown your merits as your merits, but as His own gifts."[69] Give thanks to God for your merits are His gifts.

Sin

If God has transformed your weak will into that which can merit eternal life, what can you do with your own power? Nothing but the nothingness of sin. This is what your own will, apart from the grace of God, is sufficient of itself to do. Therefore, it is pride when, finding yourself in sin, fall into

---

[68] Rule of St. Bendict, Ch. 4.
[69] St. Augustine, *On Grace and Free Will*, ch. 15.

great vexation at your propensity to evil. Rather, even then give thanks to God.

It is the mercy of God that we are saved from damnation after mortal sin. Since sin darkens the intellect, it immediately leads to more sin. If you have fallen, give thanks to God for preventing any further sin. Give thanks to God that He has revealed to you what you can do with your own power. Give thanks to God that He has given you contrition for your sins.

Final Perseverance

The grace of final perseverance is the final gift of God in this life. The Council of Trent proclaims:

> [W]ith regard to the gift of perseverance, of which it is written: *He that shall persevere to the end, he shall be saved,* which cannot be obtained from anyone except from Him who is able to make him stand who stands, that he may stand perseveringly, and to raise him who falls, let no one promise himself herein something as certain with an absolute certainty, though all ought to place and repose the firmest hope in God's help. For God, unless men themselves fail in His grace, as he has begun a good work, so will he perfect it, working to will and to accomplish (Session 6, ch. 13).

And thus canon 22 states:

> If any one saith, that the justified, either is able to persevere, without the special help of God, in the justice received; or that, with that help, he is not able; let him be anathema.

Give thanks to God that He had not revealed to you your final state. For if you were certain of eternal life, you would fall into brash presumption of mercy and commit all manner of sin. But if you were certain of damnation, you would despair and be consumed in wickedness. Either way, you would be consumed in yourself and forsake the God Who made you.

Instead, God has asked you for faith, hope, and charity. In this He has called you out of your vain desire to control the future. He has humbled you to accept His designs. He has promised you mercy and the grace to be contrite. Receive him, O man, and do not despite his gifts. Be humbled and give thanks for his merciful love.

This is why the Eucharist — *evcharistia*, "thanksgiving" — is the "the source and summit of the Christian life."[70] A humble life in accordance with the truth cannot be other than a life of gratitude to God for all things.

---

[70] *Lumen Gentium*, 11.

PART III
THE SECOND GREATEST COMMANDMENT

XV

Take Your Share
in the Sufferings of the Souls in Purgatory

The foundation of our love and devotion for the poor souls in purgatory is this: *If one member suffer any thing, all the members suffer with it; or if one member glory, all the members rejoice with it* (I Cor. xii. 26).

This is the bond of charity that binds the Church Militant to the Church Suffering and the Church Triumphant. Just as we glory in the saints and are uplifted by their victories on Earth and in Heaven, we also suffer with the souls detained in the prison of Purgatory. This is the meaning of the word "compassion": *to suffer with*. Bound to them by Christian charity, our souls burn to share in their sufferings and alleviate their burdens.

A well-known liturgical tradition bears this out perfectly: Ash Wednesday. In ancient times, a public sinner guilty of grave sin was required to do public penance in ashes for a number of years before being received again to Holy Communion. Gradually the faithful, zealous with charity, sought to place upon themselves also this penance to share the burden of their penitent brethren. As it is written, *Bear ye one another's burdens; and so you shall fulfil the law of Christ* (Gal. vi. 2). Thus did Ash Wednesday become the corporate imposition of ashes as it is today. It is this charity that must burn within us on behalf of the poor souls.

We must all be in the habit of offering penance for our brother. When any Christian sees the sins of others, he imitates Christ by offering penance for that sin. How many of us have grown angry at the sins of the clergy? How many have burned with zeal over the sins of this dark world, the offenses against

God? As the Prophet says, *the zeal of thy house hath eaten me up: and the reproaches of them that reproached thee are fallen upon me*"(Ps. lxviii. 10). Through charity, this zeal is turned into penance for their sin. Imitating Christ, the Christian offers the suffering of penance for sinners. As Isaias says, *he hath borne the sins of many, and hath prayed for the transgressors* (Is. liii. 12).

This zealous charity causes us to offer penance for the poor souls. They are now receiving the temporal punishment for their sins. Let us also take upon ourselves their punishment, in order to glorify God and free them from their bonds. There are many ways to do this. The Church incorporates this prayer at the end of every hour of the divine office: "May the souls of the faithful departed, through the mercy of God, rest in peace. Amen."

In every Mass, the faithful departed are prayed for and the merits of the Mass applied to them. There are prayers for every weekday for the poor souls, as well as the Novena for the poor souls.[71] We should all be in the habit of praying for the poor souls every day. We can also publicly pray for recently departed souls: whenever you hear that anyone has died, make the sign of cross.

The Plenary Indulgence

The most potent devotion is the plenary indulgence. The word indulgence means "kind pardon." It refers to an act wherein God, in view of the merits of Christ and the saints, grants remission of temporal punishment due to sin for some soul. In other words, God permits the saints to truly share the burden of penance incumbent upon every soul. Every sin has

---

[71] "Prayers for the Poor Souls Every Day," *Meaning of Catholic* (2019) <https://meaningofcatholic.com/2019/11/04/prayers-for-the-poor-souls-every-day/>, accessed October 25, 2023. From the *Blessed Be God* prayer book, 481-483. The Novena was written by Fr. Durin and can be accessed here: <http://catholictradition.org/Classics/novena-booklet.htm>.

its due penance (temporal punishment) to repair God's glory and cleanse the sinner from his sin. This penance is also known as "satisfaction."[72] St. Thomas speaks concerning the indulgence in this way:

> Now one man can satisfy for another[.] ... And the saints in whom this super-abundance of satisfactions is found, did not perform their good works for this or that particular person ... but they performed them for the whole Church in general, even as the Apostle declares that he fills up *those things that are wanting of the sufferings of Christ ... for His body, which is the Church* to whom he wrote (Col. i. 24). These merits, then, are the common property of the whole Church. Now those things which are the common property of a number are distributed to the various individuals according to the judgment of him who rules them all. Hence, just as one man would obtain the remission of his punishment if another were to satisfy for him, so would he too if another's satisfactions be applied to him by one who has the power to do so (Suppl. Q25 a1).

Here St. Thomas explains the logic of the indulgence in the sharing of burdens mentioned above. If we sinners can share the burdens of grave sinners with our small penances, how much more can the penances of the saints satisfy for the punishments due to sin and, yet more, the infinite merits of Christ? Thus does the Church distribute these merits gained by Christ and the saints to poor sinners of the Church Suffering.

---

[72] This satisfaction can be "partial" or "plenary." Here we will discuss only plenary indulgences, which remit all of the penance incumbent upon a soul. "Partial" remits only some.

It is His mercy that we also participate in this by gaining an indulgence.

St. Thomas then explains the method of receiving and applying an indulgence.

> That [indulgences] should be applied demands, firstly, authority to dispense this treasure; secondly, union between the recipient and Him Who merited it — and this is brought about by charity; thirdly, there is required a reason for so dispensing this treasury, so that the intention, namely, of those who wrought these meritorious works is safeguarded, since they did them for the honor of God and for the good of the Church in general (Suppl. Q25 a2).

Here he explains the union in charity and intention between God and the Church in her three parts — Triumphant, Suffering, and Militant. The indulgence is a unique manifestation of the bond of charity in the Communion of Saints. The living faithful soul unites his intentions to that of the Church authority in granting the indulgence, which unites to the saints in heaven perfected in Christ, all for the benefit of some soul in Purgatory.

From here comes the general requirements for obtaining any indulgence for the poor souls: Confession, Holy Communion, prayers for the Roman pontiff and his intentions, as well as detachment from every sin, even venial. The Confession must be completed "several days" before or after the indulgence (generally understood as eight days), which can be applied to multiple plenary indulgences. However, Holy Communion and prayer for the Roman pontiff must be completed on every day that an indulgence is obtained. Only one plenary indulgence can be obtained per day.[73]

---

[73] *Enchiridion Indulgentiarum Normae et Concessiones* (Libreria Editrice Vaticana: 2006. Third printing USCCB, 2013), 17-18.

But how can we pray for the intentions of Pope Francis when they seem to be against the Catholic Faith? As Peter Kwasniewski explains, by the nature of his office, the intentions of the Roman pontiff always include the following:

1. The progress of the Faith and triumph of the Church
2. Peace and union among Christian princes and rulers
3. The conversion of sinners
4. The uprooting of heresy[74]

Whatever other intentions may be in the mind of Pope Francis, in the supernatural order, they cannot ever contradict these. Thus, we may pray without any anxiety for the intentions of the pope to gain the indulgence.

Three common plenary indulgences available
throughout the year

Unfortunately, because charity for the poor souls has grown so cold in recent times, many of the current indulgences authorized are not accessible online to the faithful. They are contained, instead, in the *Manual of Indulgences* cited here. Fortunately, the celebrated *Raccolta* does still contain a great number of previously indulgenced prayers and practices for the faithful.[75] Here we will share three easily obtained plenary indulgences contained in the *Manual of Indulgences* currently in force.

The first is the Holy Rosary:

---

[74] Citing the *Raccolta*. Peter Kwasniewski, "Should we pray for 'our Holy Father's intentions' even if a pope has bad intentions?," *LifeSiteNews* (Oct 3, 2019) <https://www.lifesitenews.com/blogs/should-we-pray-for-our-holy-fathers-intentions-even-if-a-pope-has-bad-intentions/>, accessed October 25, 2023.
[75] Note: only currently indulgenced prayers and practiced count for the stated indulgence. The *Raccolta* is no longer current.

> A plenary indulgence is granted to the faithful
> who devoutly recite the Marian Rosary in a
> church or oratory, or in a family, or religious
> community or an association of the faithful and
> in general when several of the faithful gather
> for some honest purpose.[76]

This indulgence is granted with a few conditions in praying the Rosary itself: it must be at least one third (that is, five decades of the total fifteen, or the Luminous Mysteries), and they must be said consecutively. In public recitation, the mysteries must be announced "according to local custom," but in private the faithful may "simply join in meditation." Thus this plenary indulgence can be easily obtained by daily communicants who pray a family Rosary.

Another common indulgence is Eucharistic Adoration. A plenary indulgence is provided for "the faithful who visit the Blessed Sacrament for adoration lasting at least half an hour."[77] Make sure to use your Holy Hours to benefit the holy souls.

Finally, another simple plenary indulgence is gained by devout reading of the Holy Scriptures. This indulgence is helpful because it does not require its completion at a set location.

> A plenary indulgence is granted to the faithful
> who read Scripture as spiritual reading from a
> text approved by competent authority and with
> the reverence due to the divine word for at least
> a half an hour.[78]

Here the decree tacitly contrasts "spiritual reading" from mere intellectual study of the Holy Bible as Protestants or secularists are wont to do. Spiritual reading instead is meant in

---

[76] Ibid., 58.
[77] Ibid., 48.
[78] Ibid., 100.

the same way as one would read the spiritual classics such as the *Imitation of Christ*: slowly, devoutly, humbly, with prayer. Place yourself in the presence of God, and then read the Scriptures before Him.

These simple indulgences can easily be worked into your spiritual discipline each month, hinging on a regular confession. In gaining indulgences, we increase in charity and merit before God. This helps us overcome our own sin as well and keep eternity before our eyes. Take the time to form disciplines for the sake of the holy souls. Do not forget them. *Rest eternal grant unto them, O Lord, and let light perpetual shine upon them.*

XVI

The Poor Need Real Mercy,
Not a Marxist Fantasy

'I love humanity,' he said, 'but I wonder at
myself. The more I love humanity in general,
the less I love man in particular. In my dreams,'
he said, 'I have often come to making
enthusiastic schemes for the service of
humanity, and perhaps I might actually have
faced crucifixion if it had been suddenly
necessary; and yet I am incapable of living in
the same room with any one for two days
together, as I know by experience. As soon as
any one is near me, his personality disturbs my
self-complacency and restricts my freedom. In
twenty-four hours I begin to hate the best of
men: one because he's too long over his dinner;
another because he has a cold and keeps on
blowing his nose. I become hostile to people
the moment they come close to me. But it has
always happened that the more I detest men
individually the more ardent becomes my love
for humanity.'[79]

The spiritual truth of this passage from Dostoevsky was
once summed up to me by a spiritual father: "Naïve and
immature people have a great passion to 'serve humanity,' but

---

[79] Fyodor Dostoevsky, *The Brothers Karamazov*, trans. Constance
Garnett (New York: the Lowell Press, 1912), bk. II, ch. iv.

they cannot bear to serve a human being standing right in front of them."

This is the pervasive folly of our age, and indeed several centuries of modernity. The bloodshed wrought in the name of "humanity" is a testament to the irrationality of the modern epoch. The poor are themselves weaponized by this murderous ideology in more forms than one, and here we see the nefarious enticement as truly demonic: *Satan himself transformeth himself into an angel of light* (II Cor. xi. 14). Communism, called by Pius XI "the Satanic scourge," indeed appears as an angel of light, precisely because the miseries of the poor are real:

> The Communism of today, more emphatically than similar movements in the past, conceals in itself a false messianic idea. A pseudo-ideal of justice, of equality and fraternity in labor impregnates all its doctrine and activity with a deceptive mysticism, which communicates a zealous and contagious enthusiasm to the multitudes entrapped by delusive promises.
>
> This is especially true in an age like ours, when unusual misery has resulted from the unequal distribution of the goods of this world. This pseudo-ideal is even boastfully advanced as if it were responsible for a certain economic progress. As a matter of fact, when such progress is at all real, its true causes are quite different, as for instance the intensification of industrialism in countries which were formerly almost without it, the exploitation of immense natural resources, and the use of the most brutal methods to insure the achievement of gigantic projects with a minimum of expense.[80]

---

[80] Pius XI, *Divini Redemptoris* (1937), 7, 8.

With the reasonable severity of a true pontiff, Pius XI saw that the evil of Communism was not created *ex nihilo*, but was reacting to the real injustices caused by an excess of profiteering and exploitation of workers in the worst excesses of Capitalism (notwithstanding the material wealth created by free-market innovation and technology). The Marxist then takes a true injustice from which the poor suffer and uses the poor man's anger against injustice (which is righteous) and his envy of the rich (which is sinful) to *gain power for himself.*

From the start, the Church understood that the Marxist cares little for the poor man, but the Marxist's devotion is merely to "mankind." Marxists' love is for an ideology, not persons. This mask comes off shortly after the Communists have taken power like in Russia or China — then their true aims become evident. If they truly cared for the poor, they would not seek to the destroy the Church, which is, has been, and ever will be — as even her enemies are forced to admit — the greatest defender of widows, mother to orphans, and advocate for the poor that history has ever seen. Pius XI again:

> It may be said in all truth that the Church, like Christ, goes through the centuries doing good to all. There would be today neither Socialism nor Communism if the rulers of the nations had not scorned the teachings and maternal warnings of the Church. On the bases of liberalism and laicism they wished to build other social edifices which, powerful and imposing as they seemed at first, all too soon revealed the weakness of their foundations, and today are crumbling one after another before our eyes, as everything must crumble that is not grounded on the one corner stone which is Christ Jesus.[81]

---

[81] Ibid., 38.

Pius XI wrote these words in 1937, when the tenuous international organization, the League of Nations (forerunner to the United Nations), was about to shattered by the onset of the Second World War. The pontiff saw through the lens of history that all the efforts of modernity, no matter how vast and impressive, were nothing without the blessing and authority of His Majesty, Our Lord Jesus Christ, King of Kings. As the same pontiff had said more than a decade prior in the wake of the global bloodshed of World War I:

> [T]hese manifold evils in the world were due to the fact that the majority of men had thrust Jesus Christ and his holy law out of their lives; that these had no place either in private affairs or in politics: ... as long as individuals and states refused to submit to the rule of our Savior, there would be no really hopeful prospect of a lasting peace among nations.[82]

The fact remains that whatever politics one promotes, whatever tax system or economic stimulus package is promoted, nothing can ever replace the rule of the true king, Jesus Christ. Indeed, it was from our fathers who understood this loyalty that true mercy for the poor could be given. Men looked to the world to come, and understood that at the Judgment, the *King shall he sit upon the seat of his majesty* and separate the sheep from the goats. And He will say to the goats who neglected the poor: *Amen I say to you, as long as you did it not to one of these least, neither did you do it to me. Depart from me, you cursed, into everlasting fire which was prepared for the devil and his angels* (Mt. xxv. 41, 45).

But Christians have mercy on the poor because they have true charity. They seek to alleviate the misery of the poor

---

[82] Pius XI, Encyclical *Quas Primas* (1925), n. 1.

because they take their suffering for their own. This is an imitation of Christ, who took our sufferings for his own.

From this love of Jesus Christ and the poor for His sake — and not some malleable and murderous ideology of "mankind" — sprang the innumerable charitable works of mercy throughout the history of Christendom: innumerable saints and orders, friars, convents, hospitals, hospices, orphanages, ransomers of slaves, non-profit loan charities (the *Mons Pietatis*) — all rescuers of the poor. It is here in the bosom of the Church that the poor find *true mercy*, because they are loved as persons, not simply given a citizen's crumbs from the bread line of "the party." To speak to secular Leftists in their own language, the Catholic Church is the greatest humanitarian organization the world has ever seen. If you love the poor, then promote Catholicism. But their aims are not true mercy and charity, but merely their own ideologies.

One cannot have charity for an ideology, since an ideology is not a person. But an ideology can manipulate a group of persons by provoking their passions for some brighter future for "mankind." This pseudo-altruism propaganda began when Henry VIII, for the sake of his own lust and greed, proclaimed himself head of the Church and seized all the lands of the Church that formerly were held for the poor. They ended up in the hands of powerful nobility and other elites, and this religiously justified theft was replicated across the European countries.

The bloody mass revolutions by means of rhetoric have been going on ever since — creating innumerable widows and orphans where the bodies of all the fathers died. The tyrants who imitated Henry VIII in their contempt for the poor and the Church — Catholic and Protestant alike — were all overthrown by mass bloodshed in the name of ideologies and slogans. Marxism sprang up like weeds in this worldwide revolutionary era, and what Pius observed and predicted has come to pass: *everything must crumble that is not grounded on the one corner stone which is Christ Jesus.*

Lest any man foolishly believe that Marxism is confined to the fallen Soviet Russia or the still standing China, consider the words of John Hardon, S.J. even in 1998: "The United States of America is the most powerful Marxist country in the world."[83]

The solution for poverty must be a solution according to reality, not a Marxist fantasy. They need real Christian mercy, not a Marxist utopia that distributes starvation. Let us remember the poor and do all we can to salve their misery in the Name of Jesus Christ.

---

[83] John Hardon, S.J. "The Influence of Marxism in the United States" *Mindszenty Report* (Cardinal Mindszenty Foundation, August 1998), Vol. XXXX-No. 8.

XVII

A Short Catechism on Almsgiving

The three great works of penance are prayer, fasting, and almsgiving.[84] In this chapter, we will define the penance of almsgiving in the form of a brief catechism.

What are alms?

Alms are "every spiritual or corporal work of mercy."[85] Prümmer defines almsgiving as "a work of mercy whereby we give something to the needy for the sake of God (no. 226)."

In the Gospel, our Lord speaks of *giving alms* (Mt. vi. 3) and the words are ποιοῦντος ἐλεημοσύνην. This is literally "doing mercy" (*poiountos eleemosynen*), which uses the same root word as in the petition *Kyrie eleison* — Lord have mercy.

What is an act of mercy?

St. Thomas explains:

> A person is said to be merciful [*misericors*], as being, so to speak, sorrowful at heart [*miserum cor*]; being affected with sorrow at the misery of another as though it were his own. Hence it follows that he endeavors to dispel the misery of this other, as if it were his; and this is the effect of mercy (I q21 a3. Cf. I-II q69 a3).

---

[84] *Catechism of Pius X*, Satisfaction and Penance, q605.
[85] Ibid., q608.

Thus, "the motive for giving alms is to relieve one who is in need" (II-II q32 a1). Since "mercy is an effect of charity," almsgiving is "an act of charity through the medium of mercy" (ibid.).

What are the works of mercy?

The Seven Spiritual Works of Mercy are the following:

> To give counsel to the doubtful
> To instruct the ignorant
> To admonish sinners
> To comfort the afflicted
> To forgive offenses
> To bear patiently the troublesome
> To pray for the living and the dead

The Seven Corporal Works of Mercy are these:

> To feed the hungry
> To give drink to the thirsty
> To clothe the naked
> To shelter the needy
> To visit the sick
> To visit the imprisoned
> To bury the dead

Are corporal works greater than spiritual works?

No. St. Thomas says spiritual works of mercy excel corporal works in almost every way, except in the case where some poor man has an urgent corporal need. In this case, the corporal are better than the spiritual works since "a man in hunger is to be fed rather than instructed" (II-II q32 a5). Since acts of mercy serve the needy, the most urgent need comes first in an individual case.

Are Catholics bound to give alms to those in need?

St. Thomas considers the question of whether almsdeeds are of precept or of counsel.[86] He answers that alms are of precept:

> Some are punished eternally for omitting to give alms, as is clear from Mt. xxv. 41-43. Therefore almsgiving is a matter of precept.

> As love of our neighbor is a matter of precept, whatever is a necessary condition to the love of our neighbor is a matter of precept also. Now the love of our neighbor requires that not only should we be our neighbor's well-wishers, but also his well-doers, according to I Jn. III.18: *Let us not love in word, nor in tongue, but in deed, and in truth.* And in order to be a person's well-wisher and well-doer, we ought to succor his needs: this is done by almsgiving. Therefore almsgiving is a matter of precept (II-II q32 a5).

The Roman Catechism also makes reference to Our Lord's words in the Gospel and confirms that alms are a precept and duty:

> On the last day God will condemn and consign to eternal fires those who have omitted and neglected the duty of almsgiving, while on the contrary He will praise and introduce into His heavenly country those who have exercised mercy towards the poor.[87]

---

[86] A precept is a divine command that obliges the Catholic under pain of mortal sin. A counsel is given to the free choice of an individual soul — e.g., the evangelical counsels of poverty, chastity, and obedience.
[87] *Roman Catechism*, 3.7 Do Not Steal.

Are we bound to give to all who are in need?

No. St. Thomas observes that we are bound to love all men equally with regard to wishing them well (benevolence), but we can love with our actions (beneficence) only those who are nearby since "we cannot do good to all" (II-II q26 a6). Therefore, "we are not bound to relieve all who are in need, but only those who could not be succored if we not did not succor them" (II-II q32 a5).

Should we give alms out of what is necessary for ourselves and our families?

No. St. Thomas:

> [It] is altogether wrong to give alms out of what is necessary to us in this sense; for instance, if a man found himself in the presence of a case of urgency, and had merely sufficient to support himself and his children, or others under his charge, he would be throwing away his life and that of others if he were to give away in alms, what was then necessary to him (II-II q32 a6).

Therefore, alms should be given out of what is surplus to our necessities. Prümmer summarizes:

> The greater the need of the neighbour and the more abundant the resources of the donor, so much the greater is the latter's obligation of giving alms. On the other hand, the less severe the neighbour's need and the smaller the resources of the donor, so much the less urgent is the latter's obligation (*loc. cit.*).

145

Thus, St. Thomas outlines the circumstances wherein the neglect of alms becomes a mortal sin:

> There is a time when we sin mortally if we omit to give alms; on the part of the recipient when we see that his need is evident and urgent, and that he is not likely to be succored otherwise — on the part of the giver, when he has superfluous goods, which he does not need for the time being, as far as he can judge with probability (II-II q32 a5).

This is because, as the Apostle says, *he who does not have care for his own is worse than an unbeliever* (I Tim. v. 8). Thus, "we are bound to give alms of our surplus, as also to give alms to one whose need is extreme: otherwise almsgiving, like any other greater good, is a matter of counsel" (II-II q32 a5). St. Alphonsus says it is sufficient to give 2% of all surplus income.[88]

St. Thomas allows that only in some extreme case, when the common good is under threat, could one give away from one's own necessities "since the common good is to be preferred to one's own" (II-II q32 a6).

However, if we make only enough money for our own bare necessities, it is praiseworthy (but not obligatory) to work for the relief of the poor. The Roman Catechism says:

> If we are not able to give to those who must depend on the charity of others for their sustenance, it is an act of Christian piety, as well as a means of avoiding idleness, to procure by our labor and industry what is necessary for the relief of the poor.[89]

---

[88] Prümmer, *loc. cit.*

[89] *Roman Catechism*, loc. cit.

Pègues also observes that further obligations bind those who have great resources.

> Although there may be no pressing need for helping our neighbour, is there any strict and grave obligation to make use of the spiritual and temporal goods one has received in superabundance from God with the view of bettering our neighbour or society?
>
> Yes, one who has received spiritual and temporal goods in superabundance from God is in duty bound to act in this way.[90]

What is the spiritual effect of alms?

The Roman Catechism says that almsgiving is a "medicine suited to heal the wounds of the soul" and quotes Scripture, which speaks of the spiritual reward of alms, such as Tob. 12:9: *For alms delivereth from death, and the same is that which purgeth away sins, and maketh to find mercy and life everlasting.*[91]

Spirago discusses numerous benefits, such an remission of sins; eternal recompence; temporal blessings; bodily health; answers to prayer; and obtaining the prayers of the poor, whose "prayers have great power with God."[92] St. Thomas also says the satisfaction made by alms is even greater than that which is obtained by prayer and fasting.[93]

What about those who appear to be harmed by alms?

St. Thomas considers the case in which a needy person begs alms in order to commit sin: "We ought not to help a

---

[90] R. P. Thomas Pègues, *Catechism of the Summa* (1922), II-II 3.9.24.
[91] Roman Catechism, 4.5 Forgive Us As.
[92] Fr. Francis Spirago, *The Catechism Explained* (1899), II-A, 3.5.
[93] Ibid.

sinner as such, that is by encouraging him to sin, but as man, that is by supporting his nature" (II-II q32 a6).

Spirago discusses this further, mixing prudence with mercy:

> To give to those who are known to be idle and addicted to drink, is to encourage them in sin; but it is better to err on the side of charity than of severity[.] ...As all shipwrecked sailors without distinction are received in a port, so we should not sit in judgment upon those who have fallen into poverty, but hasten to help them in their misfortune.[94]

Why am I bound to give away my surplus if it belongs to me?

St. Thomas fields this objection and answers it as follows:

> Objection: it is lawful for everyone to use and to keep what is his own. Yet by keeping it he will not give alms. Therefore it is lawful not to give alms: and consequently almsgiving is not a matter of precept.

> Reply: The temporal goods which God grants us, are ours as to the ownership, but as to the use of them, they belong not to us alone but also to such others as we are able to succor out of what we have over and above our needs. Hence Basil says [*Hom. super Luc.* xii, 18]: "If you acknowledge them," viz. your temporal goods, "as coming from God, is He unjust because He apportions them unequally? Why are you rich while another is poor, unless it be that you may

---

[94] Spirago, *loc. cit.*

have the merit of a good stewardship, and he the reward of patience? It is the hungry man's bread that you withhold, the naked man's cloak that you have stored away, the shoe of the barefoot that you have left to rot, the money of the needy that you have buried underground: and so you injure as many as you might help." Ambrose expresses himself in the same way (II-II q32 a5).

Thus, the saints confess the common principle that, as Cahill observes, "God has ordained material things to satisfy the needs of all."[95] Therefore, even private property can come under the obligation of almsgiving in the circumstances discussed above. In other words, while you retain ownership over your private property, you do not have absolute power to use it for your own private ends at all times.

---

[95] Rev. E. Cahill, S.J., *The Framework of a Christian State* (Roman Catholic Books reprint 1932), 40.

XVIII

How to Help the Poor

When those outside the Church evaluate her according to their materialist ideologies, they are forced to admit her great material provisions for the poor and vulnerable. The so-called "Enlightenment" project was intended to outdo the Church in purely natural goods. This has failed and continues to fail as the unborn holocaust spreads its darkness across the globe. Child murder is the prime example of this failure, because the Brave New World of post-Christianity solves the problem of pain by hurting nature itself. The "solution" offered to woman is to hurt her nature and murder her child. The masculine virtue—which might seek to save the child and the mother—is dismissed as "toxic masculinity." The Marxist vision therefore is hostile to human nature, and thus it can never hope to "build back better" the fallen world because its solution is to kill human life, whether through abortion or population control.

This error redounds to hurt the poor and vulnerable. First, because the Marxist sexual revolution creates poverty. Children born out of wedlock, by definition, are born into poverty. Marriage, considered on the natural level only, is a vow of security and provision and the most powerful force against poverty. A child born to married parents is born into income security. If the Marxists really cared about poverty they would promote marriage. Instead, they switch to their second tactic: blame poverty on the political structure. This allows them to focus their effort for "change" not on themselves, but on some enemy outside themselves. Finally, the Marxist, by first creating poverty and blaming it on politics, can then whip up the mob to give him the power he desires. He can then promise the mob sexual freedom in exchange for power. This is the wicked cycle of our world right now.

But it is too easy for the Christian to critique this evil. It is too simple for us to find things to blame. Instead, we must act. We must put our faith into practice against the howls of the mob. Here let us examine the ways in which we can truly help the poor in the way the Church desires and the saints have taught us.

Face to Face

First, while the Marxist looks for answers on the highest level of politics, the Church puts her focus on an individual person. The Marxist wants to follow his ideology and avoid the individual person who is in need. The saints show us the opposite approach.

The first miracle worked by the Apostles in Acts illustrates this fundamental principle of Christian almsgiving: *a certain man who was lame from his mother's womb... when he had seen Peter and John about to go into the temple, asked to receive an alms. But Peter with John fastening his eyes upon him, said: Look upon us* (Acts iii. 2-4). Here the Apostles look at the beggar and speak to him as a person. This man is not simply a statistic or a formality to be completed on the way into the temple. A person lays a greater obligation on the believer, so that he cannot easily extract himself from the person's presence. The fundamental truth about helping the poor is that it is not merely "helping the poor" but helping a person. We must not let "the poor" become itself an ideology. Every person has individual needs and circumstances which must be addressed.

Most telling of all, Our Lord Himself tells us when He damns the goats He does so on the basis that *as long as you did it not to one of these least, neither did you do it to me* (Mt. xxv. 45). We need to extract ourselves from the Marxist sloganeering here, and truly consider the danger of our eternal damnation. When we encounter a man in need, we must follow Peter and John and all the saints, who looked at the poor man and saw Christ. St. Francis did see Christ in the poor man (Lapide, Commentary on Mt. 25:45). This fact is used by the Marxist to pursue their globalist agenda. But as early as 1926, Pius XI denounced the "purely imaginary figure of the Saint conjured up by the defenders of modern error" (*Rite Expiatis*, 1).

Instead, when we make contact with any person in need, we should treat them as we would anyone else. If you live in a city, you might see someone begging on a street corner. Applying this "face to face" principle, we might speak to a person who is asking for alms and truly "look at them." This means meet them. Find out their name. What is their situation? What do they need? This act already gives them an immense gift of charity from person to person. This is the charity that is obligatory at all times and in all places, but especially for the poor man. The Marxists want to create a vast bureaucracy and by doing so they make the individual poor person into a cog in a machine. The greatest poverty is the loss of charity, and especially the pain of being left alone. The Christian must speak to a poor man like a man.

Get to Know Your Community

The conversation then turns to the subject that the beggar started with: his need. This is where we must have the prudence to understand that a poor man's situation cannot be solved with a single monetary donation. He is out on the street for some reason that goes beyond simply money. From here, there are two actions of almsgiving, which are not mutually exclusive. On the one hand, you can give him your spare change and any excess wealth you have. On the other hand, you can identify his need and connect him with organizations that are experienced with helping those in need.

This brings us to the second necessary step for helping the poor: getting to know your community. This will allow you help someone in need. If you don't know where to start here, try this. First, you have to put yourself in the shoes of a needy person. Perhaps it is an unwed mother. Perhaps a homeless, unemployed man. Search your city for a homeless shelter. Call them and ask them: where can I find a bed for the night or a meal? Then think about what you would need in a given situation. Where can I find housing and employment help? Where can I get a drivers' license? Where can I get help with my GED? Your nearest homeless shelter will have all the connections you need. Most major cities already have a network of Christians helping the poor with resources to get employed, get housing and provide for their families.

These connections enable you to truly provide for the poor man more than your dollar. He needs more than an alms, he needs friendship and support long term. Your Christian brethren are already doing this, you just need to become aware of their work. You can also spend time volunteering at these ministries as a means of almsgiving.

Parish Ministry

Once you have some knowledge of the existing help your community gives to the poor, you can then make sure that your parish also has the resources to help the poor. Many poor people know that they can turn to the Church, and not without reason. Your parish should have connections with all the ministries in existence in order to help each individual poor person that calls the parish office.

The best model I have seen for parish ministry to the poor is that employed by the St. Vincent de Paul society. Unfortunately the lay order, like so many other orders, has lost the spirit of its founders and succumbed to Marxist Liberation Theology. But the fundamental model developed and promoted by Bl. Frédéric Ozanam, Bl. Rosalie Rendu, and Venerable Leo Dupont continues to be the best scheme for our urbanized epoch. This ministry works like this: a group of parishioners meet regularly to address the needs of the poor.

When someone in need calls the parish, this group reaches out to them and arranges a visit to their home. One or two people go to the home and meet the family. This provides the opening for a relationship of Christian friendship.

When the family is introduced and their needs identified, the friend from the parish can find and connect them with the resources necessary to succor their needs. Maybe that is the parish food pantry. Maybe that is monetary assistance. Maybe that is negotiating with a strict landlord on their behalf. The needs of an individual family can also be addressed by the group in order to decide on the allocation of time and money as each need presents itself.

Without a doubt, every parish should be known in the community for the help it gives to the poor. If someone is in need in the neighborhood, someone should be saying to them, "Call St. Michael's Church down the street, they will help you." We recall here the words of St. Paul when he described his and Barnabas' meeting with Peter, James and John, about the Gospel. *They settled on the preaching that we should go unto the Gentiles, and they unto the circumcision: Only that we should be mindful of the poor: which same thing also I was careful to do* (Gal. ii. 9-10). The Gospel proclamation has always included help for the poor. The saving of souls has always included the saving of bodies.

So many of the bishops have abandoned the Gospel in favor of Marxism. The Marxist critique is leveled against the Church by saying that Christian neglect the poor. Even though this is generally false in Church history, it is a convincing lie because there are some Christians who do neglect the poor. If we follow the saints, we can give the lie to the Marxist as an act of charity with God's help.

XIX

How to Evangelize:
Eight Things

Charity the First Truth

We cannot control things in Rome or the White House, but God has put us in a particular situation with its own responsibilities. There are people in your life whom God has given to you to love. When Our Lord is asked "Who is my neighbor?" He tells the story of the Good Samaritan who sees someone in need and shows mercy to him.

It is important to note, as we have already seen in the catechism on almsgiving, that we are not bound to help everyone in the world. We just can't do that. But the Good Samaritan helps someone he encounters on the street. The word neighbor means "the person next to you." We are not called to "love humanity" or love "all people in the world." When St. John says, *let us love in deed and not only in word*, he means *our neighbor*.

Here we come to the critical duty of all Christians to do these spiritual works of mercy:

To give counsel to the doubtful
To instruct the ignorant
To admonish sinners
To comfort the afflicted

All of these can be considered under the heading of "evangelization," because sharing the Gospel includes all of these. We must emphasize that sharing of the Gospel is indeed a work of mercy. It is an act of love to those in need: the doubtful, the ignorant, the sinner and the afflicted.

We Catholics have many truths to share with the world. But the first and most important truth to share is *love*. This is the essence of the Gospel, that God *so loved the world* (Jn. iii. 16). Those who seek to do their duty to evangelize – and we all have this duty – must begin by meditating upon what is charity.

What we note here from these four spiritual works of mercy is that they are *different things for different people*. This is because *charity seeketh not its own advantage* (I Cor. xiii. 5). We must first determine what a person needs, so that we can serve him in that way. This is how charity is the first truth to share.

This brings up the admonition of St. Thomas where he says that if a certain person may become worse if we rebuke them, then we should not rebuke them (II-II q33 a6). Somebody may be living in sin and need to hear the truth about that. But you realize that they are hardened in their hearts and to rebuke them at this point would provoke further hardening. So you realize that what they need is to know you love them. It is wise saying that *"People don't care how much you know until they know how much you care."*

On the other hand, we don't want to use this as an excuse to not tell the hard truths which can sometimes break relationships. Try to determine where a person is at spiritually, then enter into what the Holy Spirit is doing in their life *now*, instead of imposing your own ideas on their spiritual progress. Fast and pray for their openness to grace, then do what you can and leave the rest to God.

Outside the Church there is no Salvation

Now it is important to emphasize this dogma of the Church in order to undergird the reason we evangelize.[96] There are various nuances to this dogma, but the summary is included in this condemnation from the Syllabus of Errors:

> [CONDEMNED:] Good hope at least is to be entertained of the eternal salvation of all those who are not at all in the true Church of Christ.[97]

In other words, there is no reasonable hope that non-Catholics will be saved. As the Church has made clear, there is *some hope* that some of them might be saved by an implicit baptism of desire, but there is no reasonable hope for this.[98] Contrary

---

[96] "The sacrosanct Roman Church, founded by the voice of our Lord and Savior,... firmly believes, professes, and proclaims that those not living within the Catholic Church, not only pagans, but also Jews and heretics and schismatics cannot become participants in eternal life, but will depart 'into everlasting fire which was prepared for the devil and his angels' [Matt. xxv. 41], unless before the end of life the same have been added to the flock; and that the unity of the ecclesiastical body is so strong that only to those remaining in it are the sacraments of the Church of benefit for salvation, and do fastings, almsgiving, and other functions of piety and exercises of Christian service produce eternal reward, and that no one, whatever almsgiving he has practiced, even if he has shed blood for the name of Christ, can be saved, unless he has remained in the bosom and unity of the Catholic Church." Decree, *Cantate Domino*, Council of Florence, 1445.

[97] Pius IX "*Quanto conficiamur*," Aug. 10, 1863 Denzinger (43rd ed. 2865-2867).

[98] "Among those things that the Church has always preached and will never cease to preach is contained also in that infallible statement by which we are taught that 'outside the Church there is no salvation.' ...[Pius XII in *Mystici Coporis*] mentions 'those who are related to the mystical body of the Redeemer by a certain [unconscious/ ignorant] yearning and desire [*inscio quodam desiderio ac voto*]' and these he by no means excludes from eternal salvation, but who, on the other hand, as he states, are in a condition 'in which they cannot be sure of their own

to the popular narrative, Vatican II did not change this dogma.[99]

We cannot act as if non-Catholics will necessarily be saved. Since we don't have a reasonable hope that they will be saved, we must act according to what is reasonable and in our power, by God's grace. As for the other means by which God might save some, that is His affair. As for us, this dogma imposes upon us a duty.

But this is only according to your state in life. The duties of your state in life are the first priority of loving your neighbor. Raising your children in the Faith comes before evangelizing outside your family. But there are many ways to do this that do not require a lot of effort.

The Miraculous Medal

A good organization to join is the Militia Immaculata of St. Maximilian Kolbe. He carried around miraculous medals to give to people. He called them his "bullets." He was inspired by the story of the secular French Jew Alphonse Ratisbonne who was challenged to wear the miraculous medal. He went into a church in Rome and saw a vision of the Virgin Mary and was instantly converted.

The miraculous medal can work wonders of opening hearts to the Gospel. Join the Militia and carry these medals with you wherever you go. If you strike up a conversation with anyone about anything (even if religion is not brought up!) give them

---

eternal salvation' since 'they are deprived of so many and such great heavenly gifts and helps that can only be enjoyed in the Catholic Church.'...With these wise words he condemns both those who exclude from eternal salvation all united to the Church only by implicit desire and those who falsely assert that men can be saved equally well in every religion." HOLY OFFICE decree on "Feeneyism," Denzinger (43rd ed.) 3866-3873.

[99] "Whosoever, therefore, knowing that the Catholic Church was made necessary by Christ, would refuse to enter or to remain in it, could not be saved" *Lumen Gentium*, 14. See also Paul VI, *Credo*; *Ecclesiam Suam*, 64-65, 68; Holy Office, *Dominus Iesus* (2000), 22.

a miraculous medal. Leave medals at the coffee shop, restaurant, library. Wear a large miraculous medal on the outside of your clothes to tell people you are Catholic. We need to trust in supernatural means to open hearts to the Gospel.

Family, Friends, Neighborhood

The first area of influence for everyone is their family and friends. Remembering that charity is the first truth, show your closest community how much you care by your commitment to love them. Show them your commitment to your Faith by small things like praying before and after meals, abstaining from meat on Fridays, and resting on Sundays.

Meet your neighbors. Invite them over for dinner. Be kind. Place a Mary statue in your front yard. Put out a "Free library" with good Catholics books inside (besides the "great western canon").[100] Your closest community should know what you're about, and know that you mean it by your actions.

Daily Interactions

There's an opportunity to evangelize in daily interactions with strangers. There's something that is asked of us daily, often multiple times a day: "How are you?" This is an opportunity. You can say things like, "Blessed!" "Too blessed to be stressed!" "Grateful to God!" or "Glory to Jesus!"

But don't do this in a way that alienates somebody, because you also want to know and love them. Ask the cashier, "How's your shift been?" "Do you get out soon?" "Has it been

---

[100] The "great western canon" refers to a body of literature passed down from ancient times that have formed the basis for western education, from Virgil to Dante to the great works of English literature like Shakespeare. One could also include modern classics like C. S. Lewis, Evelyn Waugh, Leo Tolstoy, Fyodor Dostoevsky, Sigrid Undset, Flannery O'Connor and J. R. R. Tolkien.

busy today?" These questions tell the person that you value them as a human being, not just as a transaction.

And when you depart, don't forget something like "God bless!" or "Merry Christmas!" and such things.

Finally, remember the power of a smile. I know a close friend who smiled every day to a nearby apartment neighbor. One day she received a note on her door that said "I was about to kill myself and was going out the door to do it. But then you passed by and smiled at me and I suddenly decided against it. Thanks." It's amazing what God has planted in the human heart which can be communicated so simply as just sharing a smile.

From the Heart of the Parish

Other than these things, which everyone can do, every parish needs to have a dedicated group who evangelizes the community. This needs to be connected with the RCIA program so that the evangelization group can plug in any converts to the program to receive their catechism ahead of Sacraments. Think about it: if your parish doesn't have this, should you start it? Thankfully, there's a very good organization that you can join who can help you do this.

St. Paul's Street Evangelism

This is a lay group of solid Catholics who have chapters across the nation training Catholics to do evangelization. Their method is simple: at some public event in your community you set up their sign with Mary and Jesus and an invitation to the Gospel. You print out their tracts and have them with you. Then sit on the street corner and hand out Rosaries, miraculous medals and holy cards. You'll see that almost everyone takes these Catholic trinkets, and you can also get them blessed by the priest beforehand.

Some of these people will stop and want to talk more. Don't worry about having all the answers. Remember: charity is the first truth to share. If you don't have the answer why not invite them to meet your priest? Every community should see their local Catholic parish evangelizing the street.

Conversational Evangelism

Another method is going out in pairs to public places and striking up conversations about the Faith. What you do is you pray and fast for hearts beforehand, then you go out to some place like the food court at the mall, and find someone who seems like they would be interested in talking. Then you come up to them and say, "Hi my name is __ and this is ___. We're from ___ parish and we are talking to people about the Catholic Faith. Would you like to share your thoughts and talk about it?"

They might say no, then you say, "Ok thank you have a good one!" Or they might say yes, and you sit down and have a chat, bringing your miraculous medals.

It's scary at first, but once you do it, it becomes more easy and natural.

These and other methods are simple things that many of us can do to fulfill our duty to love our neighbor in this way and give him the spiritual works of mercy. Ask the Virgin Mary to obtain the graces necessary to take the next step in this area today.

XX

How to Love Bad Bishops and Keep the Faith

The distinction between religious submission and the assent of faith is crucial to understanding our obligations as Catholics in our time of crisis. This is what helps us love bad bishops but also keep the Faith. The key is in the distinction between the virtues of faith and piety.

The Virtue of Piety

Religious submission is rooted in the virtue of piety. This virtue does not refer to devotional practices as it is used colloquially. St. Thomas defines piety as a sub virtue to justice, which is "rendering to each one his due" (II-II q58 a1). Piety is particularly concerned with rendering to our parents and other superiors the honor due to them (II-II q101 a1). Honor means to bear witness to some excellence (II-II q103 a1). Any person in authority bears an excellence because their authority represents God Himself.

As such, part of the virtue of piety is submission, which is enjoined upon all in different ways, but is ultimately rendered to God. As it is written, *Children, obey your parents in all things: for this is well pleasing to the Lord* (Col. iii. 20), or again, *Let women be subject to their husbands, as to the Lord* (Eph. v. 22) or again *Let every soul be subject to higher powers. For there is no power but from God: and those that are ordained of God* (Rom. xiii. 1).

What does it mean to submit? The verses above, the word "submit" translates the Greek ὑποτάσσω which literally means "to arrange under" (Lat. *subdo* "to give under"). This then brings out the meaning of "religious submission of mind and will." This means to subordinate what you think and what you do to another person who holds authority over you as ordained by God. The virtue of piety causes us to render obedience to those who hold authority over us.

This is the virtue that undergirds the life of child, whose spiritual maturation is largely contingent upon his piety. The more a child reverences and listens to his parents, the more quickly he can advance in the knowledge of God. In the same way the more Catholics hold piety toward our fathers in the faith, the more we can grow in the spiritual life. As it is written, *He that walketh with the wise, shall be wise* (Prov. xiii. 20).

Thus we must understand that the virtue of piety is the foundational virtue in the natural order through which we receive the doctrines of the Church. By rendering obedience to our parents and superiors, we gain the saving knowledge of Christian truth.

The Virtue of Faith

The assent of faith comes from the virtue of faith. St. Thomas defines faith as "a habit of the mind, whereby eternal life is begun in us, making the intellect assent to what is non-apparent" (II-II q4 a1). However, whereas the virtue of piety is a natural virtue—meaning a man can gain this virtue without baptism—faith is a supernatural virtue, infused at baptism, whereby man is "raised above his nature" (II-II q6 a1). This is an action of God's grace which allows a man to believe in God and the truths about Him. These truths about Him are known as the "articles of faith." The assent of faith specifically means to assent to the articles of faith, which we will discuss below.

Thus we see the first contrast between the virtue of piety and the virtue of faith in that the former concerns submission due to human authority, whereas faith regards the divine truths of revelation. However, these two virtues are intimately connected by Tradition.

TIMOTHY S. FLANDERS

Sacred Tradition

Tradition means "a thing passed down" (Grk. παράδοσις, Lat. traditio). It refers to the whole of all things passed down to us from our fathers: doctrines, liturgies, art, music and other monuments.[101] The most important thing passed down, though, are the articles of the faith. Tradition forms the vehicle by which the faith can be handed down. The articles of faith specifically come from a variety of sources of infallibility in the Church. Contrary to the popular misconception, there are multiple sources of infallibility from which the faith springs:

1. Scripture (written Tradition)
2. Tradition (unwritten Tradition: Fathers, liturgy, creeds, monuments)
3. The consensus of the Fathers
4. The consensus of Ecumenical Councils
5. Definitive Papal pronouncements (*ex cathedra* statements)
6. The consensus of the scholastics
7. The consensus of the whole body of the faithful (*sensus fidelium*)[102]

From these all the articles of the faith are derived. These writings form of the central part of Tradition which is passed down. The assent of faith is given to what is infallibly true and "of the faith" (*De Fide*), founded solidly on these sources of infallibility.

However, the verb "pass down" implies two parties. This is where piety is needed. The passing down cannot occur unless the receiving party has piety and submits to the authority of the giver of Tradition. This starts with the Church authorities – parents and priests.

---

[101] On the monuments, see Ripperger, *Topics on Tradition* (Sensus Traditionis Press, 2013), 17ff.
[102] See Ripperger, *Magisterial Authority* (Sensus Traditionis Press, 2014), 15ff.

God endowed the Church with divine authority by which she subjects all nations to her authority in Christ by the Gospel. Every soul which subjects himself through piety to the Church receives the Sacred Tradition which includes the saving faith. As the rite of Baptism says:

Priest: What are you asking of God's Church?
Sponsors: Faith.

The Church is the authority by which the parents receive the Tradition which gives faith. If the parents did not have piety, they would not religiously submit to receive the Tradition which gives faith. The rite of Baptism is the Sacrament by which faith is infused in the soul, and the rite itself is part of Tradition.

Here we may distinguish between the articles of faith and the virtue of faith. The articles of faith are truths which can be written down, whereas the virtue is infused at Baptism which allows the intellect to assent to those truths. But the Church gives both of these by passing down the articles of faith and also giving the Sacrament which infuses the virtue.

After a child receives the virtue of faith at baptism, this faith can then grow when a child in turn has piety toward his parents, who teach him the articles of faith. *The father shall make the truth known to the children* (Is. xxxviii. 19). *Come, children, hearken to me: I will teach you the fear of the Lord* (Ps. xxxiii. 12).

It is because of piety that the loss of faith after the Second Vatican Council coincided with an iconoclastic fervor which destroyed the monuments of art, architecture and music of our fathers. If a man does not have piety to receive the faith of our fathers neither will he revere the monuments made by our fathers.

The Faith Passed Down

Here we may draw a necessary distinction between the articles of faith passed down ("tradition of the faith") and the faith expounded. First we will discuss the former. The Faith "passed down" refers to all the writings of our fathers referenced above, whereas the latter refers to the exposition of these writings as given by authorities today. Piety will have reverence for both the dead and the living, but the former is the foremost authority. The purpose of the passing down of faith is that the next generation possesses and understands these writings and the articles of faith they contain, by which they may seek everlasting life. Consider a father giving a copy of the Baltimore Catechism to his son as his own and you have a picture of what this is.

Not all teachings, however, that are passed down are of the faith (*De Fide*) and thus are binding on a man's conscience. All, however, must be received with piety as a sacred inheritance from our fathers. As Ripperger notes, following St. Bellarmine, "Violation of Tradition does not apply equally to all aspects of the tradition, but all of it binds under the pain of sin, either venial or mortal."[103] It is thus that the Church distinguishes various levels of theological certainty, which help to define what is and what is not an article of faith. These are based on the sources of infallibility listed above. The more an article of faith is based on these, the higher degree of certainty it has. These are known as the "Theological Notes," but will not be treated here.[104]

Thus through piety, the soul receives the faith passed down and adheres to it faithfully according to its Theological Note. Some things in the Tradition are not certain, and some are free

---

[103] Ripperger, *The Binding Force of Tradition* (Sensus Traditionis, 2013), 35.

[104] For more on this, see T. S. Flanders, "Theological Notes," *The Meaning of Catholic* (Aug 22, 2019) <https://meaningofcatholic.com/2019/08/22/the-meaning-of-catholic-theological-notes/>, accessed October 28, 2023.

opinions. The virtue of piety makes every soul also receive these things, not as articles of faith but with humility and reverence.

Ripperger notes:

> As a Catholic, in all matters of religion one must submit one's judgment to the judgment of the Church unless the Church in no way has pronounced judgment on the topic. However, once the Church pronounces judgment on it in any way or if there has been a discussion of that topic somewhere in the tradition, we are bound to investigate and submit our judgment to those who are higher than us in the ecclesiastical order.[105]

Thus in any article of faith or teaching, a Catholic must submit his mind and will to the Tradition of our fathers. If an authority of any kind has pronounced judgment on any matter, we are bound by piety to submit and, if it is an article of faith, we will give the assent of faith. If there is truly no judgment passed down on some matter then and only then does a Catholic have freedom to form his own opinion on anything.

The Faith Expounded

This refers to the Tradition of faith as expounded not in the writings of our fathers, but from authorities like our parents, our priest, bishops and pope. Whenever any of these authorities speak on the faith, the normal response of piety is religious submission of mind and will. This means witnessing to the excellence of their authority and subjecting our intellect to their words. It truly means to listen and consider what is said with humility. This is a crucial point as we must keep the virtue of piety at all times.

---

[105] Ripperger, *Magisterial Authority*, 46.

The faith passed down, moreover, is meant to be grasped by the faithful so that they can properly identify the articles of faith and assent to them. Thus they become *manifestly true*. For example, it is manifestly true that Our Lord was born of a virgin. This is an article of faith. Since this proposition is manifest, every Catholic holds an equal authority in relation to it. For example, the priests who questioned the virgin birth after Vatican II cannot call upon their priestly authority to oblige any Catholic to believe their heresy. The assent of faith is the most grave and binding obligation of the intellect, whereas piety is given to human authority, which can be fallible.

Thus, another way to define piety, or religious submission of mind and will is simply *obedience in all cases not manifestly sinful*. For this reason the spiritual writers all give an allowance for human error in setting aside the obligation of obedience. Thus St. Alphonsus says that we "obey our confessors in everything which is not manifestly sinful," (Serm. 4th Sun. after Easter). And again the *Roman Catechism* says that wives must yield to their husbands "a willing and ready obedience in all things not inconsistent with Christian piety" (2.7 Matrimony duties). And again regarding children, if "commands [of the parents] be wicked or unjust, they should not be obeyed, since in such a case they rule not according to their rightful authority, but according to injustice and perversity" (3.4 Parents). This provision is most aptly said by the Apostles when they disobey the human authority of the Sanhedrin: *We ought to obey God, rather than men* (Acts v. 29).

But here we must draw a crucial distinction: in the unfortunate event when a higher authority (faith) obliges us to set aside the obedience of piety, *this does not permit us to set aside the other obligations of piety*. Since piety means honor and witnessing to the excellence of an authority, even if we must disobey man in order to obey God, we must continue to witness to their authority. This means maintaining a filial or humble affection for the authority, offering prayers and penances for their errors, and remaining united to them charitably and spiritually, even if disobedience causes tensions to arise.

This becomes the most acute when we consider this passage from St. Thomas about fraternal correction, when St. Paul rebuked St. Peter, who was his superior (II-II q33 a4). He shows that in a sense the subordinate is equal to the authority in regards to the faith, but must still "reprove privately and respectfully." However, if there is an "imminent danger" to the faith, even a public rebuke may be warranted under these conditions. Thus we see how St. Thomas shows that the subordinate must hold the obligations of pious obedience at all times, except in the grave situation when imminent danger threatens the faithful. But even here, the obligation of piety means that he still has to love him and witness to his authority. That never changes.

As readers will no doubt be aware at this time, such an imminent danger threatens the faithful from many bishops, but even the Roman Pontiff himself. As such, we must receive the faith of our fathers, assent to its infallible articles, and hold tenaciously to this faith to the point of dying for it as they did. However, we must also maintain the virtue of piety, and even if we are forced to set aside obedient submission for a grave cause, we must never cease to pray and do penance for all of our superiors, that they be converted and inherit eternal life.

If we are constrained to make some public rebuke of a superior, this should provoke in our hearts a *sadness* that it must be done. Because the obligation of piety remains even in this case, there is no room for any Christian to pridefully revel in such a rebuke. Pray to Our Lady to give you this firm piety at all times, even in dark times.

PART IV
JESUS IS KING!

XXI

The Politics of the Incarnation

Every Advent we see the commercialization of Christmas. On the one hand, I can forgive the neo-pagan Marxists for the suppression of Christ—*they know not what they do*. On the other hand, Catholics, who should know better, have in recent decades anesthetized the Incarnation so as to empty it of all physical reality. The physicality of the Incarnation—that Our Lord was truly born during the reign of Caesar Augustus around the year zero—is what brings into relief all of the event's political and social ramifications.

As time has gone by I have realized this more and more. Marxists and heretics hate Mary because they hate the Incarnation. As Newman observes, they would rather accept Jesus Christ as a "poetical expression, or a devotional exaggeration, or a mystical economy, or a mythical representation"—anything but Jesus Christ, Son of Mary, Son of God.[106] This is because the political and social power in this world can be exercised either according to the authority of God (Rom. xiii. 1-7) or by means of Satan (Apoc. xiii. 12).

---

[106] John Henry Newman, "Discourse 17: The Glories of Mary for the Sake of Her Son," *Newman Reader* (National Institute for Newman Studies, 2007)
<http://newmanreader.org/works/discourses/discourse17.html>, accessed March 25, 2021.

The Socio-Political Context of the Incarnation

The event in Bethlehem was a devastating blow against the forces of evil: *the reason the Son of God was made manifest was to destroy the work of the Devil* (I Jn. iii. 8). But this was not merely in our hearts, but at the very center of society from the soul of man to the crown of the king. His birth is an attack on Satan's claim on *all principality, and power, and virtue, and dominion, and every name that is named not only in this world, but also in that which is to come* (Eph. i. 21). Thus not only do the Devils tremble (Ja. ii. 19), but also the kings: *king Herod hearing this, was troubled, and all Jerusalem with him* (Lk. ii. 3).

The Fathers understood the politics of the Incarnation. Commenting on this verse about Herod from Luke, St. Gregory the Great says "When the King of heaven was born, the earthly king was troubled because, indeed, terrestrial exaltation is confounded when celestial greatness is disclosed" (Homily 10 on the Gospel). "For," says St. Fulgentius, "this King came, not to fight against and conquer earthly kings, but, by dying, *marvellously to subdue them.* Not, therefore, was He born to be thy successor, O Herod; but that the world might faithfully believe in Him" (Sermon 1 on Epiphany). "Christ seizes not thy royalty," says St. Leo, "nor would the Lord of the universe be contented with *thy petty sceptre.* He, whom thou wishest not to be king in Judæa, reigns everywhere, and thyself wouldst reign more prosperously if thou wouldst be subject to His sway" (Lapide).

But before Herod, Caesar was the first one to propagate his "Gospel" across the Roman Empire as "Son of God," "Lord," and "Savior," decades before our Lord was born.[107] This why God's army announces the King: *And suddenly there was with the angel a multitude of the heavenly army, praising God, and*

---

[107] For more on this Roman and Persian imperial propaganda, see T. S. Flanders, *City of God vs. City of Man* (Our Lady of Victory Press, 2021), 27-49.

saying: Glory to God in the highest; and on earth peace to men of good will (Lk. ii. 13-14). This is why St. Mark's Gospel attacks Caesar's existing propaganda, already decades old: *The beginning of the gospel of Jesus Christ, the Son of God* (Mk. i. 1).[108]

Not only that, but the nearby Persian imperial propaganda too, proclaimed their king as "King of Kings and Lord of Lords," a title which the Son of God also claimed for Himself in His final Revelation (Apoc. xvii. 14; xix. 16; cf. I Tim. vi. 15)

The Socio-Political Consequences

Christ is King and He possesses *all authority in heaven and on earth* (Mt. xxiii. 18). He claims dominion over kings, governments, presidents, laws, customs, economies, families and souls. There is nothing in the universe not claimed by His sovereignty. And this is why the temporal authority of the Church has always been the flashpoint of heretical controversy. The Kingdom of Christ is the Holy Spirit (as we discuss below) Who Incarnates the Church as the Mystical Body of Christ.[109] This is why Pope Gelasius rebuked the schismatic Roman Emperor with his famous words about "two swords" during the Acacian Schism.[110] This is why the Greek heresies all attacked the Incarnation, as Solovyov adroitly summarizes:

> The fundamental truth and distinctive idea of Christianity is the perfect union of the divine and the human individually achieved in Christ, and finding its social realization in Christian humanity, in which the divine is represented by the Church, centered in the supreme pontiff,

---

[108] Floyd Schneider, *Mark Challenges the Aeneid* (Wipf & Stock Publishers, 2019).
[109] Cf. Pope Pius XI, *Quas Primas*, 12.
[110] See Flanders, *City of God vs. City of Man*, 147ff.

and the human by the State. This intimate relation between Church and State implies the primacy of the former, since the divine is previous in time and superior in being to the human. Heresy attacked the perfect unity of the divine and the human in Jesus Christ precisely in order to undermine the living bond between Church and State, and to confer upon the latter an absolute independence. Hence it is clear why the emperors of the Second Rome, intent on maintaining within Christendom the absolutism of the pagan State, were so partial to all the heresies, which were but manifold variations on a single theme:

Jesus Christ is not the true Son of God, consubstantial with the Father; God has not become incarnate; nature and mankind remain cut off from divinity, and are not united to it; and consequently the human State may rightly keep its independence and supremacy intact. Constantius and Valens had indeed good reason to support Arianism.[111]

The Incarnation is the beginning and end of redemption from the heart of man to society and politics. It begins with *the Logos was made flesh and made his tabernacle among us and we saw his glory* (Jn. i. 14).[112] This "tabernacle" referred to the prophecy of Amos about the resurrection of the Davidic Kingdom which the Council of Jerusalem dogmatized (Acts

---

[111] Solovyov, *Russia and the Universal Church*, 14-15.
[112] The Greek for "made his tabernacle" here is ἐσκήνωσεν which the New American Bible (Rev. ed.) notes is the same Greek word used in Apoc. 21:3 – the "tent" or "tabernacle," referring to the tent of meeting from Exodus.

xv. 1-xvi. 4).[113] The tabernacle was understood as the sovereign rule of God present among men, symbolized by the construction and miraculously manifested by the glory of God. The Incarnation as God's tabernacle kingdom was typified by Moses's construction (Ex. XXVI-XL), the temple made by Solomon (III Kngs vii. 13-9:3), and the prophesies of Ezechiel (Ez. XL-XLVIII) and Aggeus (Ag. ii. 7-10), among many others.

The Son of God became incarnate to destroy the work of the devil and set up the tabernacle kingdom where God would reign with and in man. This is why the consummation of the world ends with the tabernacle begun at Bethlehem: *Behold the tabernacle* [σκηνὴ] *of God with men, and he will dwell with them* (Apoc. xxi. 3). Having destroyed the pride of kings with great wrath (Apoc. VI-XX), God finalizes His rule with His finished tabernacle. This is why the Good Friday Liturgy prays "for the holy Church of God; that our Lord and God may deign to give it peace, *subjecting to it principalities and powers.*" The presidents, prime ministers, and kings of this world must be subject to the Church. Otherwise they will not serve Christ the King but the will of man and of Satan. In Euro-America today we feel the force of this latter will more and more.

The Experiment of "Not Christmas"

This phrase about subjecting authorities to the Church was censored from the New Liturgy because the Church was attempting to pursue a new approach to Modernity. As Maritain in 1966 celebrated the end of the age of Christendom, "every vestige of the Holy Empire is today liquidated[.]"[114] Or

---

[113] Scott Hahn and Curtis Mitch, eds., "Kingdom Restoration," *Ignatius Study Bible: New Testament* (San Francisco, CA: Ignatius Press, 2010), 233.
[114] Jacques Maritain, *Peasant of the Garonne*, trans. Michael Cuddihy (New York: Holy, 1966), 4.

as Paul VI said, the Pope "neither wants to nor ought to exercise henceforth any power other than that of his spiritual keys."[115]

The idea of Maritain and Paul VI had already been advocated by James Gibbons in the 1870s shortly after the Papal States were seized by Liberals: when the Church and State are too closely aligned, the State ends up controlling the Church.[116] This is a valid concern and like Maritain we cannot disagree when he says concerning Christendom that its "grave defects" are "incontestable."[117] That the brutality of barbarism was never fully eradicated from our Christian fathers no one can dispute. And from Constantine and Charlemagne to Michael III, Philip the Fair, Henry VIII and Napoleon, kings have always sought to control the Church.

But we are at the point to consider the barbarity of a world without Christ's explicit authority proclaimed by the kings of this world. We are at the point to consider whether Pius XI was correct when he said during the First Sexual Revolution (following the Great War, the "Suicide of Europe"): "these manifold evils in the world were due to the fact that the majority of men had thrust Jesus Christ and his holy law out of their lives; that these had no place either in private affairs or in politics."[118]

Following the Second American Civil War (1861-1865) the citizens of the United States have sought nineteen times to amend the Constitution to acknowledge His Majesty.[119] This is because they believed that the Liberal revolution of removing from society the public homage due to the King was a grave error bound to erode the fundamental fabric of politics,

---

[115] Paul VI, *Discourse to the Roman Nobility*, Jan. 14, 1964.
[116] James Cardinal Gibbons, *Faith of our Fathers*, 110th ed. (New York: P. J. Kennedy & Sons, 1917), ch. 17.
[117] Maritain, *loc. cit.*
[118] Pius XI, *op. cit.* On the "First Sexual Revolution," see Flanders, *op. cit.*, 377-395.
[119] This was the work of the "National Reform Association." On the American Civil War as the "Second Civil War," see Flanders, *op. cit.*, 338-340.

society and the family. At best, the experiment of the Conciliar Church and its Liberal rapprochement is an effort to convert "Modern Man" to His Majesty by the tender "medicine of mercy." At worst, it is an experiment in "Not Christmas," pretending that Christ did not become Incarnate on earth as King, and that the Church is not His Mystical Body to whom all governments must be subject in faith and morals, and the reign of Christ is *merely spiritual*, not fleshly, earthly and incarnate. We are at the point where Catholics must truly "read the signs of the times" and choose which of these efforts is the will of God, for the will of Satan is already manifest.

Therefore, Catholic families can take this annual opportunity to meditate as a family on the kingship of Christ every Christmas. There are so many Christmas customs that celebrate the newborn King, and these customs help to give children the joy of Christ's Kingship even before they fully understand it. For adults in our time, we can look at the fact that Christ came as a little, helpless child in the face of worldwide evil. In dark times we want something big and impressive, but the Christ child proclaims His kingdom from a manger. Let us receive this kingdom with confidence, even if it seems to be very small and weak. For in the darkest point of the year comes the light of Christmas. This is the way God works.

XXII

Ascending His Throne:
the Meaning of Ascensiontide

On Ascension Thursday every year the faithful enter the season of "Little Advent," the Lord's own novena given to the apostles: Ascensiontide. Just as in winter Advent, the Church waits in joyful and fearful expectation for the Lord's coming in the flesh, the Little Advent of Ascensiontide awaits a mysterious and unknown power promised by the God-Man. The Lord commanded us to make this novena to be accomplished when He said in St. Luke: *I send the promise of my Father upon you: but stay you in the city till you be endued with power from on high* (Lk. xxiv. 29). And again in the epistle of the Feast:

> He commanded them, that they should not depart from Jerusalem, but should wait for the promise of the Father, which you have heard (saith he) by my mouth. For John indeed baptized with water, but you shall be baptized with the Holy Ghost, not many days hence (Acts i. 4–5).

Here we see a parallel at the end of Our Lord's public life to the beginning of His public life, at which time John testified: *[H]e that shall come after me, is mightier than I, whose shoes I am not worthy to bear; he shall baptize you in the Holy Ghost and fire* (Mt. iii. 11). The inauguration of the Kingdom of God is about to begin with fire, but we will return to this below. Our Lord has *come to destroy the work of the devil* (I Jn. iii. 8). Therefore, as the Easter Sequence *Victimae paschali laudes* says:

> *Death and life contended*
> *in a spectacular battle:*
> *the Prince of life,*
> *who died,*
> *reigns alive.*

He has come as King to conquer the Kingdom of Satan and establish the Kingdom of God.[120] Before He can take possession of His Kingdom, He had to fight and overcome the false king. As St. Paul says elsewhere: *that, through death, he might destroy him who had the empire of death, that is to say, the devil: And might deliver them, who through the fear of death were all their lifetime subject to servitude* (Heb. ii. 14–15). Satan is the false king who holds the *empire of death*; His Majesty Jesus Christ is the true King who, coming to the mountain of Ascension and *despoiling the principalities and powers, he hath exposed them confidently in open shew, triumphing over them in himself* (Col. ii. 15). Therefore, as the King Who has now conquered and subdued the empire of death, He says:

> All power is given to me in heaven and in earth. Going therefore, teach ye all nations; baptizing them in the name of the Father, and of the Son, and of the Holy Ghost. Teaching them to observe all things whatsoever I have commanded you: and behold I am with you all days, even to the consummation of the world (Mt. xxviii. 18–20).

---

[120] See Chris Plance and T. Flanders, "The Kingship of Christ as the Essence of the Gospel," *The Meaning of Catholic* (May 18, 2020) <https://www.youtube.com/watch?v=7LZq_urBU8g>, accessed October 28, 2023.

All power once held by the false king has now been given to the rightful heir to the throne — the Davidic ruler who is Justice Incarnate. Conquer the nations, he says, therefore, and extend my rightful authority over the whole Earth — but not by conquest of the sword, as the Muhammadans will do, but by the power of truth and charity. In this way, the kings who formerly worshiped the false king would then worship the true King. St. Augustine:

> The gospel of Christ was preached in the whole world, not only by those who had seen and heard Him both before His passion and after His resurrection, but also after their death by their successors, amid the horrible persecutions, diverse torments and deaths of the martyrs, God also bearing them witness, both with signs and wonders, and divers miracles and gifts of the Holy Ghost, that the people of the nations, believing in Him who was crucified for their redemption, might venerate with Christian love the blood of the martyrs which they had poured forth with devilish fury, and the very kings by whose laws the Church had been laid waste might become profitably subject to that name they had cruelly striven to take away from the earth, and might begin to persecute the false gods for whose sake the worshippers of the true God had formerly been persecuted.[121]

The little novena of the Ascension is the transition from the kingdom of Satan to the Kingdom of God. The King ascends His throne and commands *his ambassadors* (II Cor. v. 20) to announce His reign to His newly received subjects throughout the world. Give them the good news, He says, that

---

[121] St. Augustine, *City of God*, Bk. 18, ch. 50.

the reign of Satan is at an end. Give them the good news that their slave master has been driven out. *Do not fear him who can kill the body* (Mt. x. 28), for since I have overcome death, the kings who worship Satan and rule by means of his power of death will be forced to bow before me. The kings will be subject to me, even as I am named *King of Kings and Lord of Lords* (Apoc. xix. 16). I have broken the power of death, therefore these false viceroys of Satan no longer have any power over you. This is why the apostles must complete the novena of the Ascension, because they must have *power from on high* in order to face down the empire of death.

At the Ascension, the apostles know that the Kingdom is at hand, for they ask: *Lord, wilt thou at this time restore again the kingdom to Israel?* (Acts i. 6). But St. John Chrysostom explains that "they had not any clear notion of the nature of that kingdom; for the Spirit had not yet instructed them."[122] And Venerable Bede says that "the disciples, who were still materially minded, believed that, since the resurrection of Christ had been accomplished, the kingdom of Israel would come immediately" (*Catena Aurea*). For yet as the King had spoken to them for forty days *of the Kingdom of God* (Acts i. 3), He had also said before His final battle with Satan (Gospel of the Fourth Sunday after Easter):

> I have yet many things to say to you: but you cannot bear them now. But when he, the Spirit of truth, is come, he will teach you all truth. For he shall not speak of himself; but what things soever he shall hear, he shall speak; and the things that are to come, he shall shew you (Jn. xvi. 12–13).

Therefore, it is the Holy Ghost who makes effective the reign of Jesus Christ the King and communicates the full truth about the nature of this rule. Just as in the Incarnation the King

---

[122] St. John Chrysostom, Homily II on Acts.

is born by the Holy Ghost, so after He has despoiled the kingdom of the false king and ascended His throne, the Holy Ghost liberates His subjects from the false king so that the True King can possess His domain. The first liberation is a liberation from falsehood, the illumination of the mind. *Then you shall know the truth and the truth shall set you free* (Jn. viii. 32).

But this reign is not just in our hearts. Pius XI: "If, therefore, the rulers of nations wish to preserve their authority, to promote and increase the prosperity of their countries, they will not neglect the public duty of reverence and obedience to the rule of Christ."[123] There are only two kingdoms: the false kingdom of Satan and the True Kingdom of Jesus Christ. Rulers cannot legitimize their rule if they refuse to acknowledge the True King. For they must then serve the false king — *He that is not with me, is against me: and he that gathereth not with me, scattereth* (Mt. xii. 30). As St. Augustine said above, the kings who formerly served the false king Satan and his demons must be subjected through the Gospel to the True King, and thus liberate their subjects from slavery to Satan.

We see two errors regarding the Kingship of Christ that are answered by the Ascension novena and Pentecost. On the one hand, the disciples look for a merely earthly kingdom. They seek the kingdom of Israel alone, but the King of Kings has received *all power in heaven and on earth — all peoples, tribes, and tongues shall serve him: his power is an everlasting power that shall not be taken away: and his kingdom that shall not be destroyed* (Dan. vii. 14). It is not merely material; rather, it *destroys the work of the devil*, that false ruler of the false kings — the fallen angel by which the kings of this world rule by the power of death.

Since the spiritual power behind these kings is broken, so too is their illegitimate rule on this Earth. Thus, on the other hand, His rule is not merely spiritual — *thy kingdom come on*

---

[123] Pius XI, *Quas Primas* (1925), 18.

earth as it is in heaven. The rule of Christ is indeed extended by the preaching of the Gospel, not Muhammadan conquest. Yet the kings must acknowledge Him, for *he is the Lord thy God, and him they shall adore* (Ps. xliv. 12). And again, *all the kindreds of the Gentiles shall adore in his sight. For the kingdom is the Lord's; and he shall have dominion over the nations* (Ps. xxi. 28–29). Even Vatican II teaches that "men and socieites" have a "moral duty ... toward the true religion and toward the one Church of Christ" (*Dignitatis Humanae* 1) and calls this "traditional Catholic doctrine."

Our Lord ascends His throne in Heaven to show that His kingdom is not of this world — not merely material. Yet He sends the Holy Spirit to make His rule is effective on Earth as it is in Heaven — not merely spiritual, so that every kingdom and government in this world may bend the knee to the Holy Name of Jesus. These are the deeds of our fathers, who by the Holy Spirit fearlessly converted emperors and kings who reigned through death and built that great civilization called Christendom.

Every Ascensiontide, let us remember eleven men and the Virgin Mary, waiting for the promised power from on high, and marvel at how this power changed the world forever. The King still sits upon His throne, sending His power from on high. Therefore, let us not worry about the world crumbling before us, nor become despondent about the Church and the crisis. *Seek ye therefore first the kingdom of God, and his justice, and all these things shall be added unto you* (Mt. vi. 33).

Whatever happens, Jesus is on the throne.

XXIII

The Kingdom of God is the Holy Spirit

At the Pentecost Octave, the Church celebrates an end and a beginning. It is the close of the Paschal cycle, which celebrates the close of the Old Covenant. This is the beginning of the Time after Pentecost, celebrating the birth of the Church under the New Covenant *not of the letter, but of the Spirit* (II Cor. iii. 6).

From Advent to Christmas to Lent, Easter, and the Ascension, Our Lord accomplished the work of establishing the New Kingdom of God. We may recall here the words of the Epistle at the Ascension: *The former treatise I made, O Theophilus, of all things which Jesus began to do and to teach* (Acts i. 1). From Advent to Pentecost, Our Lord's work was *only beginning*. And again His Majesty has declared: *Amen, amen I say to you, he that believeth in me, the works that I do, he also shall do; and greater than these shall he do, because I go to the Father* (Jn. xiv. 12). Therefore we see in Pentecost and thereafter the work of Jesus Christ continued in His Body, the Church. Just as Our Lord was incarnate of the Holy Spirit, so too we sinners, like Mary Immaculate, say "fiat": *let it be done to me according to thy word* (Lk. i. 38)

We may speak, then, of the Season of Advent and Christmas of a season of the virtue of hope — first, of Our Lord's coming in the flesh (and at the end of time), then in His infancy, the hope of His salvation to the world. This closes the season with Simeon's words of hope in the last words of the Gospel at Candlemas: *A light to the revelation of the Gentiles, and the glory of thy people Israel* (Lk. ii. 32). This phrase points to Pentecost, as we shall see.

Through Lent, Passiontide, Paschaltide, and the Ascension, we recite the most important events in our creed, thus we see an emphasis on faith. This is the foundation of our hope for eternal salvation, since our King accomplished the work of despoiling the prince of darkness in order to establish his rule. This work is the object of our faith. *For if thou confess with thy mouth the Lord Jesus, and believe in thy heart that God hath raised him up from the dead, thou shalt be saved. For, with the heart, we believe unto justice; but, with the mouth, confession is made unto salvation* (Rom. x. 9–10). This faith must *believe unto justice* in order to be a saving faith; as His Majesty said, *he that believeth in me, the works that I do, he also shall do.* We have been strengthened in our foundation, and now we must work.

Thus we find in Pentecost the longest season of the year, named for the Gift of God, the Holy Ghost. As we will discuss in the next chapter, the Holy Spirit is particularly identified with Charity. He is Charity Himself, who directs the Church corporally and individually in every Christian. This direction is so that the faith and hope engendered may not be sterile in the Christian soul, but may produce charity. These are the greater works of Jesus Christ. *Neither circumcision availeth any thing, nor uncircumcision: but faith that worketh by charity* (Gal. v. 6), and again, *if I should have all faith, so that I could remove mountains, and have not charity, I am nothing* (I Cor. xiii. 2).

It is by this charity of the Holy Ghost that Jesus Christ becomes the light of revelation to the Gentiles. Our Lord Himself closed His ministry at Jerusalem, having only occasional contact with the Gentile world. But His Majesty said, *I have yet many things to say to you: but you cannot bear them now. But when he, the Spirit of truth, is come, he will teach you all truth* (Jn. xvi. 12). There were indeed *many things* Our Lord knew could not be borne by the apostles at that time. But the Holy Spirit, Who is Charity, enkindled at Pentecost that "fire within us that should never be quenched," as Guéranger puts it. This fire of charity burned for souls, first among the Jews and then among the Gentiles. It was this fire of charity that made the Jewish Christians not scorn the heathen converts at Antioch, but marvel at the mercy of God: *having heard these things, they held their peace, and glorified God, saying: God then hath also to the Gentiles given repentance unto life* (Acts xi. 18).

It is not the earthly kingdom of Israel that is established by the Holy Ghost. He establishes the reign of Christ the King in the Kingdom of God. As Augustine says, "two cities have been formed by two loves: the earthly by the love of self, even to the contempt of God; the heavenly by the love of God, even to the contempt of self."[124] Thus it is in the Holy Ghost, Who is Charity, that the reign of Christ is made effective. An early Greek variant in the text of the Our Father according to St. Luke replaces *thy kingdom come* with *"thy Spirit come upon us and sanctify us."*[125] And again the King says, *The kingdom of God is within you* (Lk. xvii. 21), and again *if I by the Spirit of God cast out devils, then is the kingdom of God come upon you* (Mt. xxii. 28).

Since this Kingdom is founded on Charity Himself, not on force of arms like the Muhammadan false kingdom, it is truly *within you.* It is when the soul freely accepts the Gospel that the King drives out the devils from her, that He may reign by the Spirit of God. But, as we discussed about Ascensiontide, if this Kingdom of God is just in our hearts, then we have accepted a Gnostic dualism and abandoned Christ crucified in the flesh.

Rather, the Kingdom of God is a *fundamentally political loyalty.* He is the King of Kings. The heathen or Jewish convert forsakes his former blasphemy — *we have no king but Caesar* (Jn. xix. 15) — and *by the Holy Ghost says Jesus Christ is Lord* (I Cor. xii. 3). Caesar belongs to his true Lord, and he also must be made subject to His awful majesty, *our great God and savior, Jesus Christ* (Tit. ii. 13). *Give to God*

---

[124] St. Augustine, *City of God*, Book 14, ch. 28.

[125] Nestle-Aland, eds. *Novum Testamentum Graece et Latine* (Deutsche Bibelgesellschaft, 1986), 195.

what is God's (Mk. xii. 17) — and our King has taken possession of His universal Kingdom by the Holy Ghost. Therefore, give to Caesar what is Caesar's, but give Caesar himself to the One to Whom he belongs.

Our King came *to set fire upon the earth* (Lk. xii. 49), and this is the fire of charity in the Holy Ghost, by Whom the nations are made subject freely to the true King, the Gospel of His reign is announced, and souls are freed from slavery to the *empire of death* (Heb. ii. 15). Therefore, *say ye among the Gentiles, the Lord hath reigned. For he hath corrected the world, which shall not be moved: he will judge the people with justice* (Ps. xcv. 10). For *all the gods of the Gentiles are devils: but the Lord made the heavens* (Ps. xcv. 5). Repent and *bring ye to the Lord, O ye kindreds of the Gentiles, bring ye to the Lord glory and honour... Let all the earth be moved at his presence* (Ps. xcv. 8–9). *May all the kings of the earth give glory to thee* (Ps. cxxxvii. 4). And may the Church say: *We give thee thanks, O Lord God Almighty, who art, and who wast, and who art to come: because thou hast taken to thee thy great power, and thou hast reigned* (Apoc. xi. 17). *Not with an army, nor by might, but by my spirit, saith the Lord of hosts* (Zech. iv. 6).

XXIV

The Season of After Pentecost

During the long time of Sundays after Pentecost, it is easy to forget that this season is also a great season of the Church. We consider Advent, Christmas, Lent and Paschaltide as the special moments in the Church's calendar, but the season of After Pentecost can sometimes be considered not a season at all, or the Church simply "passing the time" to the next special season. Indeed, this mentality shows up in the Novus Ordo, where these Sundays have lost all signification by the banal title *Tempus Per Annum* ("Time through the Year"), or, even worse, the English title "Ordinary Time." As if the *wrestling against the rulers of the world of this darkness* (Eph. vi. 12) were a banal pastime.

Rather, this season, according to the great liturgist Guéranger states that is "a season when holy Church reaps the fruits of that holiness and doctrine, which those ineffable mysteries [of Christmas and Easter] have already produced."[126] It is "the season that is under the direction of the Holy Ghost." He explains:

> In order to give solidity and permanence to the image of Christ formed within us, it was necessary that the Holy Ghost should come, that so he might increase our light, and enkindle a fire within us that should never be quenched. This divine Paraclete came down from heaven;

---

[126] *Liturgical Year*, Volume X, Chapter 2: The Mystery of the Time After Pentecost.

he gave himself to us; he wishes to take up his abode within us, and take our life of regeneration entirely into his own hands. Now, it is during the period called, by the Liturgy, *The Time after Pentecost,* that there is signified and expressed this regenerated life, which is to be spent on the model of Christ's, and under the direction of his Spirit. [127]

Therefore the Christian may see here by the very name of *After Pentecost* as focusing on the "Gift of God Most High," the very life of God Himself in the Third Person of the Blessed Trinity, the Holy Ghost. This is shown in a number of ways. It is a season particularly emphasizing, first, the virtue of charity. While Advent and Christmas particularly highlight the virtue of hope, and Lent and Paschaltide rehearse the mysteries of the virtue of faith, the season of After Pentecost, since it is dedicated to the Holy Spirit, shows a particular emphasis on the greatest virtue, charity.

The Holy Ghost as Charity

The saints tell us that the Holy Spirit is particularly identified with charity itself. St. Paul says *the charity of God is poured forth in our hearts, by the Holy Ghost, who is given to us* (Rom. v. 5). St. Thomas describes the Holy Spirit as the love proceeding from God, which explains His Name as "Spirit" or "Ghost:"

> [T]he name spirit in things corporeal seems to signify impulse and motion; for we call the breath and the wind by the term spirit. Now it is a property of love to move and impel the will of the lover towards the object loved. Further, holiness is attributed to whatever is ordered to

---

[127] Ibid.

191

God. Therefore because the divine person proceeds by way of the love whereby God is loved, that person is most properly named The Holy Ghost (I q36 a1).

He continues, therefore, by saying that "love" is truly the proper name for the Holy Spirit Himself, quoting St. Gregory who says "The Holy Ghost Himself is Love."

The name Love in God can be taken essentially and personally. If taken personally it is the proper name of the Holy Ghost; as Word is the proper name of the Son... [T]here are two processions in God, one by way of the intellect, which is the procession of the Word, and another by way of the will, which is the procession of Love.... [T]he Father, by the Word or the Son, speaks Himself, and His creatures; and that the Father and the Son love each other and us, by the Holy Ghost, or by Love proceeding (I q37 a1, a2).

Therefore we may say that the procession of the Son is particularly tied to the intellect, that is, to truth; whereas the procession of the Spirit is particularly tied to the will, that is, to charity. Thus truth and charity become, as St. Thomas says, the "form [foundation] of all good works."[128] Thus we must do good works in charity by the Holy Ghost, and in the Name of Jesus Christ the truth.[129] This is why Leo XIII calls charity "the special mark of the Holy Ghost."[130]

---

[128] St. Thomas Commentary on Ephesians 4:15

[129] Here we must note that we are speaking in the sense of the spiritual life and the virtues, not making dogmatic statements about the Holy Trinity. All Three Divine Persons always act as one God, yet, as St. Thomas here shows, there is a disinction especially bearing on the spiritual life of the Christian soul.

[130] Leo XIII, *Divinum Illud Munus* (1897), 9

The Holy Ghost as Gift

St. Thomas further explains the saying of the Blessed Apostle quoted above regarding the Holy Ghost as Gift.

> [A rational soul] is made partaker of the divine Word and of the Love proceeding, so as freely to know God truly and to love God rightly... Hence the rational creature alone can possess the divine person. Nevertheless in order that it may possess Him in this manner, its own power avails nothing: hence this must be given it from above; for that is said to be given to us which we have from another source. Thus a divine person can "be given," and can be a "gift" (I q38 a1).

The Christian soul receives God the Holy Ghost as a gift so that man can become a *partaker of the divine nature* (I Pet. i. 4). Thus we see another aspect of the nature of love in the Holy Ghost, that of gift. St. Thomas explains thus that the Holy Ghost is also called Gift by this very nature.

> [A] gift is properly an unreturnable giving... and it thus contains the idea of a gratuitous donation. Now, the reason of donation being gratuitous is love; since therefore do we give something to anyone gratuitously forasmuch as we wish him well. So what we first give him is the love whereby we wish him well. Hence it is manifest that love has the nature of a first gift, through which all free gifts are given. So since the Holy Ghost proceeds as love... He proceeds as the first gift. Hence Augustine says (*De Trin.* xv, 24): "By the gift, which is the Holy Ghost, many particular gifts are portioned out to the members of Christ" (1 q38 a2).

Therefore the Person of the Holy Ghost Who is shone forth during this season is first Love Itself, and because of this is Gift. It remains for us to examine then the ways in which the Holy Ghost forms the soul of the Christian by His work and His gifts.

The Gifts of the Holy Ghost

Leo XIII explains the role of the Holy Spirit in the Christian soul as the Gift of God:

> The beginnings of this regeneration and renovation of man are by Baptism. In this sacrament, when the unclean spirit has been expelled from the soul, the Holy Ghost enters in and makes it like to Himself. *That which is born of the Spirit, is spirit* (Jn. iii. 6). The same Spirit gives Himself more abundantly in Confirmation, strengthening and confirming Christian life; from which proceeded the victory of the martyrs and the triumph of the virgins over temptations and corruptions... He not only brings to us His divine gifts, but is the Author of them and is Himself the supreme Gift, who, proceeding from the mutual love of the Father and the Son, is justly believed to be and is called "Gift of God most High."[131]

What are gifts of the Holy Ghost? St. Thomas explains that these are "habits whereby man is perfected to obey readily the Holy Ghost" (I-II 68 a3). In order to be united to God, the Holy Ghost must give to us the power to obey Him. The gifts of the Holy Ghost are identified in Isaias chapter XI:

---

[131] Leo XIII, *Divinum Illud Munus* (1897), 9.

> And there shall come forth a rod out of the root
> of Jesse, and a flower shall rise up out of his
> root. And the spirit of the Lord shall rest upon
> him: the spirit of wisdom, and of
> understanding, the spirit of counsel, and of
> fortitude, the spirit of knowledge, and of
> godliness. And he shall be filled with the spirit
> of the fear of the Lord (Is. xi. 1-3).

St. Thomas explains the role of each of these gifts in the
spiritual life in the Summa I-II q68. These gifts go beyond the
natural or theological virtues, since the virtues operate by
perfecting human reason. If we have the gifts of the Holy
Ghost, He can then move us not by enlightening our reason,
but by divine inspiration into our hearts.

> Now it is manifest that human virtues perfect
> man according as it is natural for him to be
> moved by his reason in his interior and exterior
> actions. Consequently man needs yet higher
> perfections, whereby to be disposed to be
> moved by God. These perfections are called
> gifts, not only because they are infused by God,
> but also because by them man is disposed to
> become amenable to the Divine inspiration.

This inspiration exceeds the mode of the natural and
theological virtues because there are times "where the
prompting of reason is not sufficient," even with the light of
faith. St. Thomas again explains why this is:

> Whether we consider human reason as
> perfected in its natural perfection, or as
> perfected by the theological virtues, it does not
> know all things, nor all possible things.
> Consequently it is unable to avoid folly and
> other like things... God, however, to Whose

knowledge and power all things are subject, by His motion safeguards us from all folly, ignorance, dullness of mind and hardness of heart, and the rest. Consequently the gifts of the Holy Ghost, which make us amenable to His promptings, are said to be given as remedies to these defects.

The great spiritual master of the twentieth century, Fr. Reginald Garrigou-Lagrange (1877-1964) explains that "the seven gifts of the Holy Ghost are in all the just."[132] In a helpful chart explanation, he sums up the traditional Thomistic teaching on the Gifts as perfecting the virtues in the soul in relation to their particular objects:

The gifts perfect — the understanding enlightened by faith / the will and the sensitive appetites — corresponding virtues

		gift of	corresponding virtues
for the penetration of truth........	understanding	faith
to judge { divine things...........	wisdom	charity
created things..........	knowledge	hope
our actions............	counsel	prudence
relative to worship due to God....	piety	religion
against the fear of danger.........	fortitude	
against disorderly concupiscences..	fear	temperance

Leo XIII extols the Gifts as essential to the life of grace:

By means of them the soul is furnished and strengthened so as to obey more easily and promptly His voice and impulse. Wherefore these gifts are of such efficacy that they lead the just man to the highest degree of sanctity; and of such excellence that they continue to

---

[132] Garrigou-Lagrange, *Three Ages of the Spiritual Life* (Herder: 1947), Vol. 1, 67.

exist even in heaven, though in a more perfect way. By means of these gifts the soul is excited and encouraged to seek after and attain the evangelical beatitudes, which, like the flowers that come forth in the spring time, are the signs and harbingers of eternal beatitude.[133]

Besides the seven gifts, Leo XIII also discusses other acts of the Holy Ghost which prompt the soul in various ways by

secret warnings and invitations, which from time to time are excited in our minds and hearts by the inspiration of the Holy Ghost. Without these there is no beginning of a good life, no progress, no arriving at eternal salvation. And since these words and admonitions are uttered in the soul in an exceedingly secret manner, they are sometimes aptly compared in Holy Writ to the breathing of a coming breeze, and the Angelic Doctor likens them to the movements of the heart which are wholly hidden in the living body. "Thy heart has a certain hidden power, and therefore the Holy Ghost, who invisibly vivifies and unites the Church, is compared to the heart" (III, q7 a1, ad 3).[134]

Thus we see that the Holy Ghost is Love Itself, Who is a Gift Himself and also gives His own gifts and inspirations to the heart of the pious soul.

---

[133] *Divinum Illud Munus*, 9.
[134] Ibid.

The Fruits of the Holy Ghost

Garrigou-Lagrange says that the gifts prepare a soul for the promptings of the Holy Ghost "as sails prepare a ship to follow the impulse of a favorable wind."[135] We may then say that the Fruits of the Holy Ghost—charity, joy, peace, patience, longanimity, goodness, benignity, mildness, fidelity, modesty, continence, and chastity (Gal. v. 22)—are the movement of the ship reaching its destination. Jordan Aumann says the fruits "give testimony that one is being guided by and is obedient to the Holy Spirit."[136] A fruit is a thing which occurs after a certain growth has occurred. For this reason the name is given since they are "highly perfected virtuous acts" which produce a "spiritual delight."[137] This delight is not mere emotion, but a foreshadowing of eternal beatitude. Juan González Arintero (1860-1928) puts it this way:

> If these works are so perfect, abundant and permanent that one is found to be in the state of producing them with facility and perfection, then they are so joyful and delightful that they constitute, as it were, a prelude to eternal happiness. Although they may be performed at the cost of annoyance and tribulation, yet they produce in us an ineffable joy to which nothing in this life can be compared. They are truly comparable to the joys of heaven.[138]

Thus the fruits of the Holy Ghost are shown in the words of Our Lord: *Blessed are ye when they shall revile you, and persecute you, and speak all that is evil against you, untruly, for my sake: Be glad and rejoice, for your reward is very great*

---

[135] Garrigou-Lagrange, *op. cit.*, 72

[136] Jordan Aumann, *Spiritual Theology* (Sheed and Ward: 1980), 98

[137] Ibid.

[138] John G. Arintero, *The Mystical Evolution*, trans. Jordan Aumann (Herdr, 1949), Vol I, 275-276, quoted in Ibid., 98.

in heaven. For so they persecuted the prophets that were before you (Mt. v. 11-12). It is above all joy in sufferings that shows the fruits because the soul that suffers with joy is detached from the things of this world and united to Christ Crucified.

What about the Charismatic Gifts?

This brings us to the modern controversy regarding the Charismatic movement. The charismatic gifts are mention by St. Paul:

> God indeed hath set some in the church; first apostles, secondly prophets, thirdly doctors: after that miracles: then the graces of healings, helps, governments, kinds of tongues, interpretations of speeches (I Cor. xii. 28).

The charismatic gifts refer to these extraordinary and miraculous abilities sometimes given to the souls of the saints. However, even though they appear to be the greatest gifts, they are in fact the lowest. Garrigou-Lagrange contrasts the ordinary gifts of the Holy Ghost with the charismatic gifts:

> This grace of the virtues and gifts is also more precious than the gift of miracles or of tongues or of prophecy; for these charismata are, so to speak, only exterior, supernatural signs, which can point out the way that leads to God, but cannot unite us to Him as sanctifying grace and charity can.[139]

External gifts are indeed the *lesser* gifts of the Holy Ghost, since they do not work an interior transformation or union with

---

[139] Garrigou-Lagrange, *op. cit.*, 78.

God. This is why the Apostle continues his passage quoted above on the charismatic gifts by saying

> be zealous for the better gifts. And I shew unto you yet a more excellent way. If I speak with the tongues of men and of angels, and have not charity, I am become as sounding brass, or a tinkling cymbal. And if I should have prophecy and should know all mysteries and all knowledge, and if I should have all faith, so that I could remove mountains, and have not charity, I am nothing (I Cor. xii. 32-xiii. 2).

The context of the most famous passage on charity is St. Paul explaining how much more excellent is charity than the charismatic gifts. Therefore it is very foolish to seek charismatic gifts as any sort of spiritual goal. And indeed, as the example of the saints shows us, they are a burden because of the attention they attract with its associated dangers to vainglory.

Unfortunately some seek out charismatic experiences as a means for spiritual consolations. But the fruits of the Holy Spirit are perfected in sufferings, since true spiritual joy is found in God alone. The saints loved to suffer for Christ, and this is the work of the Holy Ghost.

Thus the way of all the saints is in the cross of suffering by which the soul is removed from this world and united to Jesus Christ. If some of them were given charismatic gifts, they used them for the sake of God's glory and the salvation of souls. But never did they seek out extraordinary gifts and experiences. Consolations can even become an attachment, and, at worst, a nefarious deception of the Devil. This is why the saints teach us to refuse visions and extraordinary phenomena to guard against pride. Dom Lorenzo Scupoli (1530-1610) summarizes the wisdom of the saints in these words:

If our persistent foe, who never ceases to persecute us, should assail us disguised as an angel of light, stand firm and steadfast even though cognizant of your own nothingness, and say to him boldly: "Return, miserable one into your realms of darkness; for I am unworthy of visions, nor do I need anything but the mercy of my Saviour, and the prayers of Mary, Joseph and all the Saints."

And though these visions seem to bear many evidences of having been born in Heaven, still reject them as far as it is within your power to do so. And have no fear that this resistance, founded as it is on your own unworthiness, will be displeasing to God. For if the vision be from Him, He has the power to make the same known to you, and you will suffer no detriment; for He Who gives grace to the humble does not withdraw it because of acts which spring from humility.[140]

Thus it is that a soul who experiences anything extraordinary in the spiritual life should be treated with caution. And even if is divine, it is beyond one's worthiness. One should manifest it to a good priest who will give the soul objective judgment on the matter. Until then, the safest course of action, as Scupoli and the saints tell us, is to distrust these things and not seek after them.

Conclusion

The Holy Ghost has been poured out upon our souls as the Love proceeding from God Himself. He is Charity Himself. Because of God's infinite mercy, He has come to dwell with

---

[140] Dom Scupoli, *The Spiritual Combat*, ch. 66.

us in His very life. By adhering to the wisdom of the Fathers, we can know God in the Holy Spirit Who will empower us to overcome our sins and prepare us for eternal happiness. Let us love and thank the Holy Spirit and call upon Him for aid in the season After Pentecost.

XXV

Restore June to the Sacred Heart of Jesus:
Ten Things

Every June, Catholics can feel a great sadness or anger at what this month has become. Yet this is an opportunity for all of us to find positive ways to celebrate this month and reach out to non-Catholics with love.

Love is really the whole theme of the month. The greatest love: the Sacred Heart of Jesus.

In the Lord's Providence, He has already charged June with the liturgical power necessary to soften hardened hearts, and save souls and societies.

June begins with the Apostles Fast and includes the Octave of Corpus Christi, placing the Sacred Heart in the center of the month. After that comes the summer bonfire for St. John (that proto-martyr for marriage!) and Peter and Paul, ending in First Vespers of the Feast of the Precious Blood (whose collect is an invocation against demons). These are all opportunities to allow the Sacred Heart to fill us with His love, so that we can love others in this opportune month.

1. Restore the Apostles Fast in your Domestic Church and Parish

We wonder why there is so much demonic activity in our society. Actually, His Majesty has already explained that: a demon of *this kind is not cast out but by prayer and fasting* (Mt. xvii. 20).

Let's consider this: when God's people go astray and become lukewarm in penance, He permits His people to be overcome by evil for a time. Read the Holy Scriptures (start with Judges). Read the message of Fatima.

This is how this works.

The answer is simple, but not easy. If we do not do penance, God will continue to pour out His wrath until we do. Therefore, brethren in Christ, hear the word of the Lord from the greatest of Prophets:

> Ye brood of vipers, who hath shewed you to flee from the wrath to come? Bring forth therefore fruit worthy of penance. And think not to say within yourselves, We have Abraham for our father. For I tell you that God is able of these stones to raise up children to Abraham. For now the axe is laid to the root of the trees. Every tree therefore that doth not yield good fruit, shall be cut down, and cast into the fire (Mt. iii. 7-10).

I know fasting is hard – that's the point. But don't worry, you can join a lay sodality to do it together with other Catholics from around the world![141] Fasting has a long tradition in Christendom of being done *together* to strengthen ourselves to complete it, and to corporately petition God.

But what is the Apostles Fast? It's one of the things that God gave us in June centuries before June became what it is.

One of the most ancient features of June is the great feast of Peter and Paul. This is a universal feast on June 29, in both the Latin and Greek rites. In the Greek rite it includes a significant fast of preparation from Monday after Trinity through the Vigil of Ss. Peter and Paul, June 28. This fast is not as strict as Lent, and the Latin custom was always a local custom (like St. Michael's or St. Martin's Lent).

If you can't make the whole month, you can still do something, and just add a little for the Apostles Fast every

---

[141] For example, the Fellowships of St. Anthony and St. Nicholas.

June: add Wednesday abstinence to Friday this year. Next year, add Mondays too, etc.

It's better to attempt some fasting for penance and reparation with good intent and fail, than to do nothing during June. We have to make reparation to Almighty God for sins committed in June, which cry to heaven for vengeance.

And this fast is a perfect opportunity – in the month of the Octave of Corpus Christi before the Feast of the Precious Blood! – to offer fasting as *Eucharistic Reparation*.[142]

2. Exercise your Parental Conscience

Our children must grow up knowing what June is all about. In fact, they should feel excited every year for this great month because of what you tell them and what you do as a family this month. As Dr. Joseph Shaw notes in his important text, "what they fear is thousands of little platoons of families fighting against them."[143] It's easy as a mustard seed.

What I need to stress here is that parents have a duty to form their children in the Faith and educate them, which creates a corresponding right – given directly from God to the parent – to protect their children from demonic attack. Just as Our Lord loves children best, the demons hate children the most, consumed with envy that they will inherit the thrones in heaven lost by the them.

Therefore, O Parents, understand your rights and duties before God, then *do what your gut instinct tells you to do*, for the sake of your children. Obviously you should follow the law, but you should also *disobey unjust laws.*

It is for parents to rule and Christianize temporal society, and this is confirmed by Vatican II (see *Lumen Gentium, Apstolicam Actuositatem*, and even *Gaudium et Spes*). So parents should excerise their conscience in doing what they think is best in their family, community and politics.

---

[142] Join the Crusade of Eucharistic Reparation: onepeterfive.com/crusade.

[143] Joseph Shaw, *The Liturgy, the Family, and the Crisis of Modernity: Essays of a Traditional Catholic* (Os Justi Press, 2023), 278.

3. Lay People can Form Lay Sodalities

Lay sodalities and confraternities have always been the backbone of Christianizing the temporal order – Guilds themselves arose from these.

Once you've committed to something in your domestic church – fasting, reparation, boycotts, etc. – the next step is to form a lay sodality in your parish.

So what is a lay sodality?

It's merely a group of lay people who organize regular prayer and pious works on their own initiative. Remember what Vatican II says about lay groups: "The laity must not be deprived of the possibility of acting on their own accord."[144] God willing, you have a priest who can support your lay sodality. But if not, carry on with your sodality, and understand this is your right and duty directly from God by your Confirmation.

4. Lay People can Lead their own Processions

Again, God already dedicated June to marches in honor of His Eucharistic Heart. We've been doing this for centuries. We are deeply grateful that more bishops are finally promoting Corpus Christi Processions. But this is just the beginning. We need lay-led processions more and more, with or without clerical involvement. This is a strong tradition in Christendom, along with all sorts of pageantry and plays, put together by the lay sodalities and Guilds.

So once you have your lay sodality set up, why not organize a procession during the Octave of Corpus Christi (which leads up to the feast of the Sacred Heart) in honor of Christ the King? June is a great opportunity to enthrone the Sacred Heart in your home.[145] After this, you can enthrone

---

[144] *Apostolicam Actuositatem*, 24.
[145] Matthew Karmel, "Family Enthronement of the Sacred Heart," *OnePeterFive* (Jun 24, 2022) <https://onepeterfive.com/enthronement-of-the-sacred-heart/>, accessed October 28, 2023.

Him in the "liturgy of the streets." Make Banners, crosses, learn a bunch of hymns, then process down main street and show everyone the *splendor of truth*! I guarantee you – even Protestants will thank you for this.

5. Retake God's Glorious Sign from Satan

This brings us to something that to me, seems *essential* to include in the banners and signs that you make for your procession: the rainbow. Not the Satanic, inverted rainbow, but *God's rainbow.*

He instituted it Himself. *It belongs to Almighty God for thousands of years.*[146]

It appears in Genesis as a promise of God's provision, and again in Revelation as a part of His reign: *and there was a rainbow round about the throne, in sight like unto an emerald* (Apoc. iv. 3).

One of the most conspicuous features of this glorious sign of God – in contrast to its Satanic inversion – is that it is curved. This is how it appears in the natural world (besides the fact that the true sign has seven colors, unlike the Satanic version which only has six, tellingly).

So make a banner with a curved rainbow and Jesus on the throne. If you do a procession for the Sacred Heart in June and fly this banner, everyone will take notice. And the fallen angels will hate it.

6. Reach out to your friend or family member now who identifies as "LGBT"

At this point in this article let's take a step back and marvel at how Jesus Christ revealed His Sacred and Eucharistic Heart to us and created this month for His glory. For it is this Heart,

---

[146] Peter Kwasniewski, "The Glory of the Christian Rainbow and the Satanism of Its Inversion," *OnePeterFive* (May 31, 2023) <https://onepeterfive.com/christian-rainbow/>, accessed October 28, 2023.

wounded for our transgression, that softens every evil heart – starting with our own. His Heart is the *lover of souls*, Who leaves the ninety-nine sheep to go to find the one lost sheep and rejoices to find him; Who sheds his Precious Blood to save us. O how precious and loved is *one single soul created by God!*

We must remember that the people who march in "Pride parades" are *persons formed in the image of God.* They desperately need the love of the Sacred Heart. It may seem impossible to reach someone like this, but just reach out in faith and let Jesus Christ do the work. These people need love and compassion – that's the first truth they need to hear and feel, much like the rest of us. They need someone who is willing to be their friend and love them no matter what. Then you can tell them the whole truth, if their hearts are open to it.

Don't forget – against the lies of James Martin – that the Church has done this for decades (with success!) in the apostolate known as *Courage International.* This helps souls who struggle with Same Sex Attraction (SSA) and other such afflictions, with the love of the Sacred Heart. If you do know someone who has an open heart to facing their SSA as a faithful Catholic, direct them here to Courage and keep Christian friendship with them.

7. Observe the Octave of Corpus Christi

The feast of the Sacred Heart was revealed by Christ to be directly connected to this Octave, which also resulted, logically, in the Feast of the Eucharistic Heart of Jesus, and Bishop Athanasius Schneider has expressed his desire with his crusade for a "Day of Reparation for Crimes Against the Most Holy Eucharist" in each diocese as the octave day of Corpus Christi.

So June revolves around, and hinges on, this Octave. Again, just because Ven. Pius XII tragically suppressed this Octave, does not mean lay people are obliged to abandon it as well. There are many ways to celebrate the octave, and you can restore old customs (and make up your own new ones!) for your domestic church, lay sodality and parish. But here's some ideas right now:

- Go to Eucharistic Adoration (or at least visit Him in the Tabernacle) every day during the Octave
- Pray the short or long prayer of Eucharistic Reparation every day with your family and/or sodality (onepeterfive.com/crusade)
- Organize an event in your parish during the octave – devotions, dinner, a talk
- Organize your lay-led procession for this octave
- Read, re-read, and distribute copies of the manifesto of Schneider's *Dominus Est: It is the Lord* or *The Catholic Mass*
- Do the same for Kwasniewski's manifesto of Eucharistic Reparation: *Holy Bread of Eternal Life: Restoring Eucharistic Reverence in an Age of Impiety*

8. Boycotts Have Actually Worked In the Past

Catholics have a good history in these United States (and elsewhere) of bringing the heretics to their knees by attacking their idolatry to money.

What we need here is not just public statements about a boycott, but an actual boycott. This kind of social action flows directly from the lay sodality. All you do is create a requirement that all members boycott this or that thing, and commit to it. Start in your domestic church, then go to your lay sodality, your parish, your diocese, and see where it goes from there.

If you are starting on the national level of any country, and think that you need to create a massive project, you're not thinking like a Catholic – *subsidiarity in the key*. The mustard seed will conquer Empires, as it already has in history again and again.

9. Reserve a Billboard for Next Year

This is a very expensive, but highly effective thing that you can do from your lay sodality. Raise the money to reserve one for next June. Along the same lines, create bumper stickers like "June Belongs to the Sacred Heart," etc.

10. Commit Now to a Penitential Pilgrimage

We have to seriously commit to doing the penance necessary to merit the grace for a single soul who is afflicted with SSA. Maybe you don't even know someone like this – then offer it up for someone you don't know! Read about the great Christian tradition of pilgrimage and find one now to commit to every year. Or go to Holy Communion every Friday in June for the same intention. In fact, if you haven't already completed the First Friday devotions, let June's First Friday be a Holy Day of Opportunity! If you've already completed this devotion, commit to *every First Friday* for the rest of your life and offer it up for this intention and for those who have not done this devotion.

XXVI

The Obligation of Sunday Rest

The obligations of the Third Commandment are twofold: Sunday Mass and rest from work (II-II q122 a4 ad3). In our day pious Catholics are chiefly occupied in following this commandment with Sunday Mass, but the obligation to rest has been greatly obscured. Therefore here we will treat on the obligation of Sunday rest and discuss the origins of the commandment, its purpose, specifics of moral theology, and the history of why this obligation has been obscured.

Mosaic Law and the Three Types of Commandments

On pain of death, the Israelites were commanded by God to cease from work every seventh day (cf. Ex. xxxi. 15). This may seem harsh, but we need to understand that the surrounding societies (and later the Roman Empire as we will see) were "free market" economies with few moral limits of work for laborers and slaves. The masters were able to grind workers into long hours seven days per week with little rest. The idea of a weekly Sabbath limited the economy of Israel with this check upon human greed, exhausting burdens, and limitless profit. This day belonged to God in a specific way, by disallowing man to work for himself by the Mosaic law.

Jesus Christ was the New Lawgiver, higher than Moses (Dt. xviii. 15; Ps. ix. 21). Nevertheless, He said that He came *not to abolish the law, but to fulfill it* (Mt. v. 17). This meant that the typology and foreshadowing contained in the Mosaic law would find its true meaning in the New Law of Jesus

Christ.[147] St. Paul says the Mosaic laws are *shadows of the things to come, but the body is Christ* (Col. ii. 17). Christ Himself casts a shadow as it were, and that shadow is the Mosaic law. But when the body appears, the shadow is not destroyed but simply finds its true meaning. In other words, the Mosaic law still participates in the reality of the New Law.

In order to see how this affected the Third Commandment, we need to understand the three types of Mosaic law. What are these three types? St. Thomas explains that the Mosaic law contains moral law, ceremonial law, and judicial law.

The moral laws are "precepts about acts of virtue" which can never be changed, since they come from natural and divine law (I-II q99 a2). An example of this is the Ten Commandments. The Church upholds these laws as coming from God. Our King also perfects them by the New Law as with the Fifth and Sixth Commandments on the Sermon on the Mount (Mt. v. 21-28).

The ceremonial laws are those which "refer to Divine worship (I-II q99 a3)." An example are the laws contained in Leviticus for the rituals of the Aaronic priesthood and sacrifice. This priesthood was a shadow and type of the priesthood of Jesus Christ and His sacrifice, as St. Paul explains at length in his epistle to the Hebrews.

Finally, the juridical laws are "determinations of the justice to be maintained among men (I-II q99 a4)." An example of this are the penalties imposed by certain precepts, just as the death penalty for breaking the Sabbath or committing adultery. The Church adjudicates the juridical process in canon law, which may also correspond to civil law in Catholic countries as we will see.

---

[147] The term "type" is used by the New Testament (I Pt. iii. 21) and the Fathers to denote something which is not only a symbol but a participation in the reality signified. See Flanders, *Introduction to the Holy Bible for Traditional Catholics* (Our Lady of Victory Press: 2019), 42-43, 303-313.

Thus we see that the whole substance of the Mosaic law finds fulfillment in the Church's upholding of divine precepts, liturgical legislation as well as canon and civil law. This is the meaning of the Mosaic law being "fulfilled." No such fulfillment exists in Talmudic Judaism or Protestantism.

Saturday Sabbath to Sunday Lord's Day

Now the Fourth Commandment concerning the Sabbath is one part moral and one part ceremonial. St. Alphonsus explains:

> Although it is of divine and natural law that some determined time is designated to worship God, nevertheless the determination of this worship, and of the days in which it must be furnished was from the arrangement left to the Church by Christ. Then the Pope could discern that the observance of Sunday should endure only for some hours, and that some servile works would be lawful[.]... And as a result, this precept, inasmuch as it is an exhibition of worship, is indeed divine but insofar as it is a determination of the cult and time, it is ecclesiastical [ceremonial].[148]

The meaning of the Saturday rest became a shadow of our Lord's resting in the tomb, and pointed to the Resurrection day of Sunday (II-II q122 a4 ad1). Therefore because the Third Commandment was both moral and ceremonial, the ceremonial obligation tied to Saturday was transferred to Sunday, which then retained the moral obligation formerly held for Saturday. This may have been transferred by the

---

[148] St. Alphonsus, *Moral Theology*, Vol. II Bk. IVa, translated by Ryan Grant (Mediatrix Press, 2017), 286. Cf. *Summa Theologica*, II-II q122 a4 ad1.

Apostles themselves as the New Testament makes mention of *the Lord's Day* (Apoc. i. 10). However, as St. Thomas observes, because the Lord's Day is not figurative as the Sabbath was, its prohibition on work is less strict (II-II a122 a4 ad4). The Church then retains the authority to legislate the ceremonial and juridical precepts regarding the Third Commandment in the New Covenant. Moreover, this also applies to the fixing of Holy Days as we will see.

The Obligation to Rest

St. Thomas explains that "man abstains from other works on the Sabbath day in order that he may occupy himself with works connected with God's service" (II-II q122 a4 ad3). Therefore the obligation to rest from work is directly tied to the other obligation to assist at Mass. It is our resting from work so that we may worship which is a "spiritual refreshment, by which man's mind is refreshed in God" (II-II q122 a4 ad1). Thus the resting from work chiefly regards what is known as "servile work," which St. Thomas defines as works "whereby one man serves another" (II-II q122 a4 ad3). St. Alphonsus defines it as work done "by the body and ordered immediately to the advantage of the body" and thus "more advantageous to the body than to the powers of the soul."[149]

Prümmer elaborates on these principles in the modern context by distinguishing four types of work: servile (as defined above), cultural, ordinary and judicial/commercial. Cultural work is chiefly that of the mental faculties and developing the mind such as reading, writing and prayer. Ordinary work is that which is necessary for daily maintenance like cooking. Judicial and commercial work regards "public trading, such as sitting in court, defending criminals, buying,

---

[149] St. Alphonsus, *op. cit.*, 293.

selling, leasing, etc."[150] The obligation of rest, then, applies to servile, judicial and commercial work, but not to ordinary and cultural work (even if profit may be involved).[151] This is due to the nature of the work itself, being that cultural work cultivates the mind and soul, and ordinary work simply maintains what is absolutely necessary for sustenance.

But just as the Church has authority to dispense with the obligation to hear Mass, she also dispenses for grave cause the obligation to rest, for instance in grave necessity for the poor or by certain custom.[152] Moreover some occupations cannot avoid work on Sundays, such as doctors or law enforcement.

The Theology of Rest

Yet Sunday is more than simply an obligation. When we consider the spiritual side of rest, it becomes more profound. Let us consider, for example, that God has ordained that roughly one third of our entire life will be spent asleep. There is a spiritual wisdom here. When we are resting, we are *resting in Our Father's arms*. We are trusting in Him to take care of things. We are in the hands of Providence. We are letting going of our pride which tells us that we must *worry about many things*. There innumerable things in this world that we cannot control. The theology of rest seems to tell us that we must "let go and let God."

Yet sleep is a physical and emotional necessity that even materialist doctors can recognize. The rest of Sunday is a rest of a higher order. Here God calls us to "consciously sleep." When we sleep we are forced to put everything in His hands and let go our power over the whole world for a long period of the day. On Sunday, God calls us to let go again, but this time, instead of being unconscious, He joyfully invites us to *smell the flowers*. See the sunrise. Laugh with family and friends.

---

[150] Dominic Prümmer, *Handbook of Moral Thoelogy* (Roman Catholic Books reprint from 1957), 196
[151] Cf. St. Alphonsus, *op. cit.*, 296.
[152] Prümmer, *op. cit.*, 197.

Sunday tells us to get off our phones and get on our knees.
Get out of the house. Get some fresh air. Get going on a hike.
Become grateful for the beauty of this moment. Sunday rest
grounds us in the immensity of God's goodness right here right
now. It returns us to our roots – our friends and family. Food.
Play. Fun.

The profundity of this commandment has not been
explored in our day because our fathers have taken this as a
given and simply enjoyed Sunday rest. In fact, this is one of
the key aspects of Christianizing and re-Christianizing society.

Christianizing Society through Sunday Rest and Holy Days

Now as was stated above, when Our Lord came the Roman
Empire was a "free market" with no restraint for business to
impose work on Sundays for laborers and slaves. After Christ
conquered this empire and other kingdoms, the Sunday rest
began to be reflected not only in moral, ceremonial, and
canonical law, but also in civil law. This began with the first
Christian emperor Constantine, who forbade work on
Sunday.[153] The first Christianized Roman law code, the *Codex
Theodosianus*, contained this law:

> Let the course of all law suits and all business
> cease on Sunday, which our fathers have
> rightly called the Lord's day, and let no one try
> to collect either a public or a private debt; and
> let there be no hearing of disputes by any
> judges either those required to serve by law or
> those voluntarily chosen by disputants. And he
> is to be held not only infamous but sacrilegious

---

[153] Thomas Slater, "Sunday," *The Catholic Encyclopedia*, Vol. 14
(Robert Appleton Company: 1912),
<http://www.newadvent.org/cathen/14335a.htm>.

who has turned away from the service and observance of holy religion on that day.[154]

Likewise the *Codex Justianianus* in the following century: "On the venerable Day of the Sun let the magistrates and people residing in cities rest, and let all workshops be closed."[155]

But not only was the Lord's Day a day of rest, but various feast days developed and eventually became holy days of obligatory rest. This led to the sanctification of the week with religious meaning as well as the alleviation of the burden of the slave and laborer, checking the excess of those who sought only profit from their fellow human beings. Thus Cahill summarizes that during the era of Christendom, "when the social and economic life was organised after Christian ideals there was besides Sundays an average of more than one holyday of obligation every week."[156] Thus at the time of the Protestant revolt, those Catholic countries which were observant to the laws of the Church maintained a considerable leisure from work for the sake of the faith.

This began to change with the Protestant heretics, who suppressed the cult of the saints and most holy days. Since they seized Church land from the poor, they also wished to enforce more profit and production out of workers, as we see with the wicked Henry VIII.[157] This thirst for profit and suppression of religious leisure continued with the French Revolution (1789-1799), which attempted to limit the weekly rest to a nine day work week with one rest day. The first industrial revolution (1760-1840) began to threaten the workers' Sunday rest as

---

[154] *Codex Theodosianus*, C.Th. XI.vii.13,
<https://sourcebooks.fordham.edu/source/codex-theod1.asp>.
[155] *Codex Justinianus*, lib. 3, tit. 12,
<https://en.m.wikipedia.org/wiki/Blue_law>.
[156] E. Cahill, S.J. *The Framework of a Christian State* (Roman Catholic Books reprint from 1932), 401.
[157] Richard Rex, *Henry VIII and the English Reformation* (Macmillan International Higher Education: 2006), ch. 3.

well, which also threatened the poor who felt obliged to work on Sunday and many neglected the precept.

St. John Vianney and Our Lady of La Salette

In response to this widespread working on Sunday, two figures emerged in the 19th century which reacted to this. The first was the great Cure d'Ars. The Life of St. John laments that when he first came to Ars, "Servile work of every kind was done on Sunday, and at harvest time the carts and wagons were in use during the entire day 'carting souls to hell,' as Father Vianney not inaptly expressed it."[158] In response St. John launched an "unceasing war that he waged against the desecration of the Lord's day." One story relates a miracle which helped bring this about:

> One Sunday in July there was a full harvest, the wheat bending to the earth. During the High Mass a violent wind arose and threatening clouds gathered; a destructive tempest was apparently about to break. The holy priest entered the pulpit, forbade his people to touch their crops that day, and promised them a continuation of good weather sufficient for the gathering in of the harvest. His prediction was verified; the storm passed over and no rain fell for twelve days.

As a result of his tireless efforts, "The spirit of religion was revived, public worship restored, the Lord's day unusually respected and observed."

Another miraculous instance during this period (also in France) was the apparition of our Lady of La Sallette. In this vision, our Lady identified two grave sins which provoked God's wrath in bringing the potato famine of 1846:

---

[158] Anonymous, *The Life of Saint John Vianney, The Cure of Ars* (Joseph Schaefer: New York, 1911).

If my people will not submit, I shall be forced to let fall the arm of my Son. It is so strong, so heavy, that I can no longer withhold it[.]... "Six days I have given you to labor, the seventh I had kept for myself; and they will not give it to me." It is this which makes the arm of my Son so heavy. Those who drive the carts cannot swear without introducing the name of my Son. These are the two things which makes the arm of my Son so heavy[.]...

I gave you warning last year with the potatoes but you did not heed it. On the contrary, when you found the potatoes spoilt, you swore, you took the name of my Son in vain[.]...

There are none who go to Mass except a few aged women. The rest work on Sunday all summer; then in the winter, when they know not what to do, they go to Mass only to mock at religion.[159]

Some say that the famine was not as severe thanks to the revival in France helped by Our Lady of La Sallette and St. John Vianney. In any case, it must be clear that the economic changes brought about without any regard to the Third Commandment or the Church's holy days were a provocation of God's wrath.

---

[159] La Salette Missionaries, "The Message of La Salette," <https://www.lasalette.org/about-la-salette/apparition/the-story/705-the-message-of-la-salette.html>, accessed October 28, 2023.

Popes Condemn Economics which
Violates the Third Commandment

During this time of industrial revolution a number of organizations developed across nations in an effort to lobby for protection of Sunday rest. These included Protestant organizations such as the Lord's Day Alliance in North America and the Lord's Day Observance Society in the British Isles but also Catholic associations like the *Ligue du Dimanche* (League of Sunday) in Canada. These found common cause with the labor unions which sought to restrict the 12-hour working day as well.[160] Many of them were able to secure legislation in favor of Sunday rest, but many of these laws were later removed as "unconstitutional" in a secular society. But the impingement of business upon Sunday rest and other holy days was part of an overall secularization of society. At the same time, a new Industrial revolution was breaking out (1870-1914) tied to the spread of Communism, provoking the Holy See.

By 1891 Leo XIII lamented this impingement on the Third Commandment in *Rerum Novarum*:

> The working man, too, has interests in which he should be protected by the State; and first of all, there are the interests of his soul... From this follows the obligation of the cessation from work and labor on Sundays and certain holy days. The rest from labor is not to be understood as mere giving way to idleness; much less must it be an occasion for spending money and for vicious indulgence, as many would have it to be; but it should be rest from labor, hallowed by religion.

---

[160] Fahlbusch and Bromiley, *The Encyclopedia of Christianity* (Eerdmans: 2005), 787.

Rest (combined with religious observances) disposes man to forget for a while the business of his everyday life, to turn his thoughts to things heavenly, and to the worship which he so strictly owes to the eternal Godhead. It is this, above all, which is the reason arid motive of Sunday rest; a rest sanctioned by God's great law of the Ancient Covenant-*Remember thou keep holy the Sabbath day*, and taught to the world by His own mysterious "rest" after the creation of man: *He rested on the seventh day from all His work which He had done.*[161]

Thus Leo XIII began a line of popes all saying the same thing: the state must protect the Third Commandment as it had done in Christian countries. The Sunday and holy day rest is fundamental to the spiritual health of men. Pius XI:

Truly the mind shudders at the thought... when we remember how many obstacles are put in the way of the proper observance of Sundays and Holy Days; and when we reflect upon the universal weakening of that truly Christian sense through which even rude and unlettered men were wont to value higher things, and upon its substitution by the single preoccupation of getting in any way whatsoever one's daily bread. And thus bodily labor, which Divine Providence decreed to be performed, even after original sin, for the good at once of man's body and soul, is being everywhere changed into an instrument of perversion; for dead matter comes forth from

---

[161] Leo XIII, *Rerum Novarum* (1891), 40-42.

the factory ennobled, while men there are
corrupted and degraded.[162]

And again in *Divini Redemptoris*, Pius XI identified the
suppression of Sunday by the free market to be one aspect in
secularization leading to Communism:

> If we would explain the blind acceptance of
> Communism by so many thousands of
> workmen, we must remember that the way had
> been already prepared for it by the religious and
> moral destitution in which wage-earners had
> been left by liberal economics. Even on
> Sundays and holy days, labor-shifts were given
> no time to attend to their essential religious
> duties. No one thought of building churches
> within convenient distance of factories, nor of
> facilitating the work of the priest. On the
> contrary, laicism was actively and persistently
> promoted, with the result that we are now
> reaping the fruits of the errors so often
> denounced by Our Predecessors and by
> Ourselves. It can surprise no one that the
> Communistic fallacy should be spreading in a
> world already to a large extent de-
> Christianized.[163]

These things were later repeated by St. John Paul II in
Centesimus Annus after the decline of Soviet Communism and
later elaborated in *Dies Domini*:

> Until quite recently, it was easier in
> traditionally Christian countries to keep
> Sunday holy because it was an almost universal

---

[162] Pius XI, *Quadragesimo Anno* (1931), 132-135.
[163] Pius XI, *Divini Redemptoris* (1937), 16

practice and because, even in the organization of civil society, Sunday rest was considered a fixed part of the work schedule. Today, however, even in those countries which give legal sanction to the festive character of Sunday, changes in socioeconomic conditions have often led to profound modifications of social behaviour and hence of the character of Sunday.

Finally, it should not be forgotten that even in our own day work is very oppressive for many people, either because of miserable working conditions and long hours — especially in the poorer regions of the world — or because of the persistence in economically more developed societies of too many cases of injustice and exploitation of man by man. When, through the centuries, she has made laws concerning Sunday rest, the Church has had in mind above all the work of servants and workers, certainly not because this work was any less worthy when compared to the spiritual requirements of Sunday observance, but rather because it needed greater regulation to lighten its burden and thus enable everyone to keep the Lord's Day holy. In this matter, my predecessor Pope Leo XIII in his Encyclical *Rerum Novarum* spoke of Sunday rest as a worker's right which the State must guarantee[.]...

Therefore, also in the particular circumstances of our own time, Christians will naturally strive to ensure that civil legislation respects their duty to keep Sunday holy. In any case, they are obliged in conscience to arrange their Sunday rest in a way which allows them to take part in the Eucharist, refraining from work and activities which are incompatible with the sanctification of the Lord's Day, with its characteristic joy and necessary rest for spirit and body.[164]

After many decades, some protection of Sunday rest has been secured by legislation, but a religious calendar has been replaced by "the weekend" and civil holidays which honor merely earthly kingdoms. Cahill summarizes the changes that have been wrought:

> When, as a result of unchristian influences, the Church's holydays were abolished, the labourers had to work every day, in some cases every on Sundays. Later on when the demand of the organised workers for more relaxation could no longer be refused and the holidays had to be, at least partially restored, the same unchristian forces were still at work to prevent the Christian holydays from being chosen; and so purely civil holidays were established, while the Christian holydays are not regonised. Such a state of affairs is manifestly incongruous in a Catholic country.[165]

Thus we find ourselves in the state of affairs today, where numerous servile, judicial and commercial work is performed on the Lord's Day and holy days, and it is difficult for many Catholics to keep these obligations in a society and economy without moral restraint. Therefore it behooves Catholic families to keep holy the Lord's Day and fulfill the Third Commandment as much as possible. This helps create a Catholic family culture in which children can grow with the

---

[164] John Paul II, *Dies Domini* (1998), 4, 66-67.
[165] Cahill, *op. cit.*, 401.

rhythm of the liturgical calendar, and experience rest in order that they may pray and lift their minds to things heavenly, even Our Lord and King, Jesus Christ.

XVII

Last things First

There is perhaps no truth today more shunned, suppressed, and vehemently ignored than the reality of death. Modern man is consumed with indulging his slavery to his passions, proclaiming himself free, and absolutely banishing the thought that he will die. He has invented words to shun even the mention of death: "macabre," "morbid." Yet he will murder anyone who gets in the way of his slavery to his passions. The debauchery into which he throws himself keeps his vision blinded to anything but his slavery. He cannot see the one thing in the future he can never avoid or deny.

One could make a reasonable case that the historical decline in religious piety correlates with the decline in death from disease and the general modern advances in technology and comfort which obscure the reality of death. When a man can ignore death, he can ignore God. In the season most dedicated to the Four Last Things – Advent – he keeps himself distracted in his illusion with indulgence and celebrations.

Yet by God's grace, no man can ignore death forever. Eventually, a loved one dies. Eventually, a man contracts cancer or some other illness. Eventually he is face to face with what he has skillfully eluded his entire life. Then he will be confronted with this stark reality. Perhaps then he will face the difficult questions. Perhaps then he will turn to God and look over his life.

St. Francis de Sales:

Consider that then the world is at end as far as you are concerned, there will be no more of it for you, it will be altogether overthrown for you, since all pleasures, vanities, worldly joys, empty delights will be as a mere fantastic vision to you. Woe is me, for what mere trifles and unrealities I have ventured to offend my God? Then you will see that what we preferred to Him was nought. But, on the other hand, all devotion and good works will then seem so precious and so sweet: — Why did I not tread that pleasant path? Then what you thought to be little sins will look like huge mountains, and your devotion will seem but a very little thing.[166]

St. Alphonsus laments the death of sinners:

They will have recourse to God at death; but he will say to them: Why do you invoke me now? Call on creatures to assist you; for they have been your gods. The Lord will address them in this manner, because, in seeking him, they do not sincerely wish to be converted.[167]

Let not the death of a sinner overtake you. Remembrance of death is remembrance of ultimate reality. Prepare now for the fate of all flesh. Hear the words of the dead: *what you are, I once was; what I am, you will become.*[168]

---

[166] St. Francis de Sales, *Introduction to the Devout Life*, ch. 13.
[167] St. Alphonsus, *Preparation for Death*, ch. 6.
[168] This is the Latin adage *Eram quod es; eris quod sum*, which seems to have originated with pre-Christian Roman authors but has been adopted since by various saints and Catholic orders.

The Necessity of Remembering Death

Bergamo writes:

> Death is the best teacher of truth; and pride —
> being nothing but an illusion of our heart —
> clings to a vanity which it does not recognize
> as vanity; and therefore death is the best means
> by which we can learn what vanity is and how
> to detach our hearts from it.[169]

Are you angry at your brother for giving you some slight insult? Consider your death. What will become of that insult when your body is rotting in the grave and your soul is appearing before the judgment seat? Will you still hold on to your anger? Rather, the Lord says, *Unless you forgive men their trespasses, your heavenly Father will not forgive you* (Mt. vi. 14). Death cuts through your vanity to show you the emptiness of human glory.

Are you distressed about the state of the Church? Consider your death. The Lord says, *He who perseveres to the end shall be saved* (Mt. xxiv. 13). Soon you will die and face judgment. What will the Lord say you to you at that time? Did you take the talent and *out of fear bury it* (Mt. xxv. 25), or did you invest the graces given you to produce merit and save souls? Your death is near at hand, when all of these things will be stripped away from you.

As the 15th-century play *Everyman* shows beautifully, a man can take neither kindred, fellowship, goods, nor strength at death. Only good works can be brought before the judgment seat of Christ. Death causes us to see clearly the reality before us. Death causes us to see the emptiness of created comforts and place all our hope in the Uncreated. Death keeps us safe from lies, vanity, and most of all sin itself.

---

[169] Fr. Cajetan Mary da Bergamo, *Humility of Heart* (TAN reprint: 2006), 64.

Are you tempted to sin? Consider your death. Soon this empty pleasure will mean nothing at your death. Soon you will regret having taken momentary pleasure and forsaken eternal life. This transitory delight will last but an instant, while eternity will last for all time and beyond. Do not listen to the Devil, who says to you "It matters little. Tomorrow you will confess." Listen instead to your Lord who says, *Fool! This night your life shall be required of you* (Lk. xii. 20), and again, *keep watch for you know not the day nor the hour* (Mt. xxv. 13). The remembrance of death is victory over every sin.

How to Remember Your Death

Because our modern society is bent on everyone denying his death, it is extremely difficult to remember that you will die. Nevertheless, this practice is so salutary as to cause swift advancement in the spiritual life. One method is the daily remembrance. This consists of arising and making your morning offering with the consideration that you will die that very night. Say before God on the last day of your life:

Remember, O Christian Soul, that thou hast this day:
God to glorify
Jesus to imitate
The angels and saints to invoke
A soul to save
A body to mortify
Sins to expiate
Virtues to acquire
Hell to avoid
Heaven to gain
Eternity to prepare for
Time to profit by
Neighbors to edify
The world to despise
Devils to combat
Passions to subdue

229

Death to suffer
And judgment to undergo.[170]

At the end of the day make your examination of conscience while considering that you will die that night. This will bring forth true contrition for your sins, and show you the vanity of having offended your God for a trifle. Say the *Miserere*.

When lying down to sleep, lie down on your back and look to the heavens. Consider your body on its deathbed, or laid in the grave. Then place your hope in the mercy of God and repeat the prayer, *Lord Jesus Christ, Son of God, have mercy on me, the sinner.*

Another method is the monthly remembrance. Consider that this month will be your last month to live. The final day of this month will be your final day on this Earth. That night you will die.

Then look at your life and consider what you shall do before your death. Strive after virtue, and overcome your sin.

Shortly before the last day of the month, make a thorough examination of conscience. Then make your Confession as your last before you die. Then look upon your bed and say, "Will this bed be my grave? Lord Jesus I trust in Thy mercy." Then kneel and pray:

> O my God, sovereign Lord of life and of death, Who, by an immutable decree for the punishment of sin, hast determined that all men must die, behold me humbly kneeling before Thy dread Majesty, resigned and submissive to this law of Thy justice. With all my heart I detest my past sins, by which I have deserved death a thousand times; and for this cause I accept death in reparation for my sins and in obedience to Thy holy will. Yes, great God, send death upon me where Thou wilt, when

[170] Roman Catholic Daily Missal, "Subjects for Daily Meditation" (Angelus Reprint: 2004), 28.

Thou wilt, and in what manner Thou wilt. Meantime I shall avail myself of the days which it shall please Thee to bestow upon me, to detach myself from this world and to break every tie that holds me in bondage to this place of exile, and to prepare myself to appear with sure confidence before Thy judgment seat. Wherefore I surrender myself without reserve into the hands of Thy fatherly Providence. May Thy Divine will be done now and for evermore! Amen.[171]

These daily and monthly practices prepare your soul for the death that you must die. Preparing in these ways will make your inevitable death an occasion not of mourning, but of merit. Then you will do what you have rehearsed by God's grace all your life. Then you will die a good death.

The saint is not afflicted, like worldlings, at the thought of being obliged to leave the goods of this earth, because he has kept the soul detached from them. During life, he always regarded God as the Lord of his heart and as the sole riches which he desired: *What have I in heaven? and, besides thee, what do I desire upon earth? Thou art the God of my heart and the God that is my portion for ever* (Ps. lxxxii. 25, 26.).[172]

---

[171] Dom Scupoli, *Spiritual Combat* (Catholic Tradition online edition), supplemental chapter "At the Hour of Death."
[172] St. Alphonsus, Sermon XI on the Death of the Just (*Sunday Sermons* trans. Callan).

Fear of Judgment Is the Way of the Saints

Over and over in the Eastern Rite is supplication made for "a good defense before the dread judgment seat of Christ." The Apostle warns, *we must all be manifested before the judgment seat of Christ, that every one may receive the proper things of the body, according as he hath done, whether it be good or evil* (II Cor. v. 10). Thus, the saints lived.

St. Jerome: "As often as I consider the day of judgment, I tremble. Whether I eat or drink, or whatever else I do, that terrible trumpet appears to sound in my ears, arise ye dead, and come to judgment."[173] St. Augustine said nothing removed from him earthly thoughts as perfectly as the fear of judgment.[174] St. Benedict says this is the very first step in humility:

> The first step, then, of humility is if one set the fear of God always before his eyes and altogether avoid forgetfulness; and be always mindful of everything that God has ordered and always ponder over life eternal, which is prepared for those that fear God; and how hell will consume, for their sins, such as despise God; and if he keep himself at all times from sins and faults, alike of thought, of the tongue, of the eye, of the hand, of the foot, or of self-will; and moreover hasten to cut away the desires of the flesh.[175]

The fear of judgment is the way of the saints. It is the height of folly that the modern Church has cast out holy fear from our churches. Are we better than our fathers who feared

---

[173] Commentary on Matthew, quoted in St. Alphonsus, Sermon on the 1st Sunday of Advent, "On the General Judgment."
[174] Ibid.
[175] Rule of St. Benedict, ch. 7.

judgment? Do not exalt yourself above the saints, but be humbled with the fear of judgment.

Orthodox Doctrine Must Produce Holiness

You who are zealous over orthodox doctrine: beware! Let not these words of Jesus Christ be spoken of you at the Judgment:

> Not every one that saith to me, Lord, Lord, shall enter into the kingdom of heaven: but he that doth the will of my Father who is in heaven, he shall enter into the kingdom of heaven. Many will say to me in that day: Lord, Lord, have not we prophesied in thy name, and cast out devils in thy name, and done many miracles in thy name? And then will I profess unto them, I never knew you: depart from me, you that work iniquity. (Mt. vii. 21–23)

You who confess the creed of our fathers, do you imitate our fathers? You who rightly scorn the Communism of the clergy, do you have mercy on the poor? You who justly rebuke bishops for their cowardice, are you then courageous to preach the Gospel? You who burn with righteous indignation at the sins of the Holy Father, do you burn with charity also to forgive him?

As Christ says, *And his lord being angry, delivered him to the torturers until he paid all the debt. So also shall my heavenly Father do to you, if you forgive not every one his brother from your hearts* (Mt. viii. 34). Again St. John declares: *If any man say, I love God, and hateth his brother; he is a liar. For he that loveth not his brother, whom he seeth, how can he love God, whom he seeth not?* (I Jn. iv. 20).

The only thing that matters at the Judgment is *faith that worketh by charity* (Gal. v. 6). If your faith does not produce charity, then your faith is dead — merely an intellectual

233

exercise, and worse, the faith of demons (Jas. ii. 13, 26). It is at the Judgment, says St. Augustine, that the demon will stand before God and say of the sinner, "Most just God, declare him to be mine, who was unwilling to be yours."[176] Therefore, fear the Day of Judgment, and *bring forth fruit worthy of penance* (Mt. iii. 8), that these words may not be spoken to you by the Just Judge:

> Depart from me, you cursed, into everlasting fire which was prepared for the devil and his angels. For I was hungry, and you gave me not to eat: I was thirsty, and you gave me not to drink. I was a stranger, and you took me not in: naked, and you covered me not: sick and in prison, and you did not visit me...Amen I say to you, as long as you did it not to one of these least, neither did you do it to me. And these shall go into everlasting punishment: but the just, into life everlasting (Mt. xxv. 41-43, 45-46).

Speaking on the Judgment, St. Alphonsus laments the many graces wasted by Christians:

> Christians, he will say [at the judgment], if the graces which I have bestowed on you had been given to the Turks or to the Pagans, they would have done penance for their sins; but you have ceased to sin only with your death.[177]

Let not the graces given to you from your baptism be a source of shame at the Judgment, but of glory. Do penance and overcome your sin. By God's grace, do the works of mercy.

---

[176] Quoted in St. Alphonsus, *op. cit.*
[177] Ibid.

At the Judgment, the saints rejoice in the work of God in them: "O happy penance! which merited for me such glory."[178]

Fear of God and Hope in God

The Holy Ghost says the *fear of the Lord is the beginning of wisdom* (Prov. i. 7), and the Lord says *fear him* (Lk. xii. 5). And yet the Lord also says, *Fear not, little flock, for it hath pleased your Father to give you a kingdom* (Lk. xii. 32). Do not fear as the pagans who have no hope, but understand that this fear is placed in you that you may trust not in yourself, but in God, Who is rich in mercy. Therefore, fear the Lord and hope in Him, as the Prophet declares: *The Lord taketh pleasure in them that fear him: and in them that hope in his mercy* (Ps. cxlvi. 11), and again, *his mercy is from generation unto generations, to them that fear him* (Lk. i. 50).

There is perhaps no other prayer that so perfectly expresses fear and hope than the *Dies Irae* (originally an Advent hymn). The fear is drawn out in considering the Day of Judgment from the beginning of the hymn:

> *Oh, what fear man's bosom rendeth,*
> *When from heaven the Judge descendeth,*
> *On whose sentence all dependeth.*

The second half of the hymn considers the mercy of God and the Passion of Christ, bringing hope to the penitent:

> *Faint and weary, Thou hast sought me,*
> *On the Cross of suffering bought me.*
> *Shall such grace be vainly brought me?*

> *Guilty, now I pour my moaning,*
> *All my shame with anguish owning;*
> *Spare, O God, Thy suppliant groaning!*

---

[178] Ibid., St. Peter of Alcantara to St. Teresa.

Through the sinful woman shriven,
Through the dying thief forgiven,
Thou to me a hope hast given.

Worthless are my prayers and sighing,
Yet, good Lord, in grace complying,
Rescue me from fires undying.

Low I kneel, with heart's submission,
See, like ashes, my contrition,
Help me in my last condition.

Mercy is for the contrite. Fear the Lord, and your soul will burn with salutary sorrow for sin. Consider His Passion, and your soul will feel true contrition and hope in His mercy for the Day of Judgment. Suffer your penance now, that you may not suffer the words of condemnation on that day, but the blessed words of eternal life: *well done, good and faithful servant* (Mt. xxv. 23). Jesus Christ will bless the saints at the Judgment:

> He will then bless all the tears shed through sorrow for their sins, and all their good works, their prayers, mortifications, and communions; above all, he will bless for them the pains of his passion and the blood shed for their salvation. And, after these benedictions, the elect, singing alleluias, shall enter Paradise to praise and love God eternity.[179]

---

[179] Ibid.

Hell Is Proof of Man's Exalted Dignity

The Offertory prayers speak of how God "wondrously endowed dignity to human nature."[180] The eternity of Hell manifests the proof of this exalted dignity in two ways. The first is that man's soul is immortal. The only time that God still creates out of nothing is the creation of our immortal soul in the womb of our mother. By its very nature, God has made our souls eternal. The soul will exist beyond the grave. Consider this deep truth. Your very being, your very soul is truly immortal and will exist forever in eternity. But you must choose which eternity this will be: an eternity of happiness in the vision of God, or eternal torments deprived of God.

Thus, we see a second part of man's exalted dignity: his free will. The eternal destiny of your immortal soul rests on your choice before you die. This choice will determine your fate. God will not force you. "The quality of mercy is not strained."[181] God refuses to do damage to man's dignity by sending him to Heaven by force. This would destroy the essential nature of charity, which is a free act of love.

Therefore, the eternity of Hell is proof that man's immortal soul is free. In the depths of torments that await the damned, their fate still proclaims the glory of God. Meanwhile, in a society proclaiming its devotion to man's liberty and "the rights of man," eternal punishment has been removed, thus his freedom and immortality. Never before has man's dignity been so degraded in the name of that very dignity as has the empty and nefarious rhetoric of the modern epoch.

Even so, God offers pardon freely, yet the damned refuse it. In this we see their malice, as St. Alphonsus says, "The damned are so obstinate in their sins, that even if God offered pardon, their hatred for him would make them refuse it."[182]

---

[180] *Humánæ substántiæ dignitátem mirabíliter condidísti.*
[181] *Merchant of Venice*, Act IV, Scene I.
[182] St. Alphonsus, Sermon on the Eternity of Hell, 21st Sunday after Pentecost.

Against Psychologizing Hell: God Indeed Punishes Sinners

The truth that man's immortal soul freely and obstinately chooses Hell must not obscure the action of God in their regard: God punishes the damned. There are some who wish to obfuscate God's action in eternal punishment as if man is the sole arbiter of his eternal fate. Indeed, the damned *do* desire heaven — but they do not desire God. They desire to go on sinning and reap the fruit of their wickedness. To justify their iniquity, they rashly hope *all men will be saved*. The Blessed Apostle censures this folly:

> Be not deceived, God is not mocked. For what things a man shall sow, those also shall he reap. For he that soweth in his flesh, of the flesh also shall reap corruption. But he that soweth in the spirit, of the spirit shall reap life everlasting (Gal. vi. 7–8).

Some Catholics wish to forget that God said: *I will render vengeance to my enemies, and repay them that hate me* (Dt. xxxii. 41). Man is not the judge. Rather, Jesus Christ says, *I have the keys of death and of hell* (Apoc. i. 18). Against the sentimentalizing of judgment, hear the words of the Son of God:

> Be not afraid of them who kill the body, and after that have no more that they can do. But I will shew you whom you shall fear: fear ye him, who after he hath killed, hath power to cast into hell. Yea, I say to you, fear him (Lk. xii. 4–5).

It is God Who holds the power of your eternal fate. Therefore, do not follow the way of the sinner who is deceived that he can continue the mockery of God and win for himself rewards in the world to come. St. Paul thunders against the presumption of these sinners:

> For if we sin wilfully after having the knowledge of the truth, there is now left no sacrifice for sins, But a certain dreadful expectation of judgment, and the rage of a fire which shall consume the adversaries. A man making void the law of Moses, dieth without any mercy under two or three witnesses: How much more, do you think he deserveth worse punishments, who hath trodden under foot the Son of God, and hath esteemed the blood of the testament unclean, by which he was sanctified, and hath offered an affront to the Spirit of grace? For we know him that hath said: Vengeance belongeth to me, and I will repay. And again: The Lord shall judge his people. It is a fearful thing to fall into the hands of the living God (Heb. x. 26–31).

The Eternity of Hell Is Certain

More and more, heretics and sinners seek to complicate the simplicity of Hell with more speculation, theologies, historical studies, resourcing, rethinking. Yet they do not seek the only true answer to Hell: repent! As St. Alphonsus says, "[t]hese are not opinions controverted among theologians; they are dogmas of faith clearly revealed in the sacred Scriptures."[183] As it is written, *Depart from me, you cursed, into everlasting fire* (Mt. xxv. 41) and again *the smoke of their torments shall ascend up for ever and ever* (Apoc. xvi. 11) and again *they shall suffer eternal punishment in destruction* (II Thess. i. 9).

---

[183] Ibid.

If Hell were not eternal, it would not deter us from sin. It would not frighten us to repentance. The extent to which sin will blind us to its consequences cannot be overstated. In the moment of temptation, sin tells us, *No, you shall not die the death* (Gen. iii. 4), and we believe it! Indeed, the blindness of sin would cause a man to accept a punishment in order to sin if that punishment was temporary. To what lengths will sinners go to fulfill their lusts? Did not the sin of David lead him to deceit and murder? Even so, the rationalizations and justifications of sin are endless. The reasons given in time of temptation cannot be numbered.

But they fall silent in the face of the eternity of Hell. *Be silent before the face of the Lord God: for the day of the Lord is near. That day is a day of wrath* (Soph. i. 7, 15). In Hell, there is no turning back. There is no escape. *And they shall go out, and see the carcasses of the men that have transgressed against me: their worm shall not die, and their fire shall not be quenched* (Is. lxvi. 24). Jesus Christ cries out to the wicked: *You serpents, generation of vipers, how will you flee from the judgment of hell?* (Mt. xxiii. 33).

Seek Pardon Before Judgement

Yet our God does not frighten us with the fires of Hell in order that we may be damned. As He says by the Prophet:

> Be converted, and do penance for all your iniquities: and iniquity shall not be your ruin. Cast away from you all your transgressions, by which you have transgressed, and make to yourselves a new heart, and a new spirit: and why will you die, O house of Israel? For I desire not the death of him that dieth, saith the Lord God, return ye and live (Ez. 18:30–32).

The fires of Hell are shown to us so that we may escape them in the world to come. In the hardness of our hearts, the eternal flames of Hell are a mercy for sinners, to give them the necessary conversion for eternal life. Do not neglect mercy for your own soul, but meditate upon the fires of Hell. St. Thomas More prayed to "foresee and consider the everlasting fires of Hell." St. Alphonsus says:

> He who fixes his thoughts on eternity, is not elated by prosperity nor dejected by adversity; because, having nothing to desire in this world, he has nothing to fear: he desires only a happy eternity, and fears only a miserable eternity.[184]

St. Augustine observes that he who thinks on eternity and is not converted either has lost all faith or has lost all reason.[185] The day of the Lord is near at hand. Who knows how long your life will last? Be converted to the Lord, for He is merciful to forgive penitent sinners. Consider eternal life or eternal death, and do not be deceived by the momentary pleasures of this life.

> When Thomas More was condemned to death by Henry the Eighth, his wife Louisa went to him for the purpose of tempting him to obey the royal command. Tell me, Lousia, replied the holy man, how many years can I, who am now so old, expect to live? You might, said she, live for twenty years. O foolish woman! he exclaimed, do you want me to condemn my soul to an eternity of torments for twenty years of life?[186]

---

[184] St. Alphonsus, *op. cit.*
[185] Ibid.
[186] Ibid.

The Glory of Paradise

St. Benedict sums up the spiritual necessity of the Four Last Things in his chapter "What Are the Instruments of Good Works":

> To have wholesome fear of the day of judgment.
>
> With fear to shrink from hell.
>
> To long for eternal life with all spiritual desire.
>
> To have the expectation of death daily before one's eyes.[187]

Here we see pithily summarized the whole way of the saints, which has led them to great glory in holiness. Now we consider the glory of paradise, for which we must long "with all spiritual desire." The glory of this blessed country is beyond all human reckoning, yet it is the burning desire of every faithful heart. Without a doubt, "the greatest of all the torments of the damned in hell, arise from the thought of having lost heaven through their own fault."[188] The act of contrition says, "I am sorry for my sins because I dread the loss of heaven."

For the Apostle declares emphatically that *eye hath not seen, nor ear heard, neither hath it entered into the heart of man, what things God hath prepared for them that love him* (I Cor. ii. 9). Yet we must contemplate the glory of our heavenly home even if our finite contemplation falls like a drop water in an ocean. God has not left us without images to stir our spiritual longings for eternal life. Let these considerations be close to your heart so that you may stir up the necessary spiritual longing for paradise.

---

[187] Rule of St. Benedict, Chapter 4.
[188] St. Alphonsus, Sermon on the 2nd Sunday of Lent, On Heaven.

The End of Sin and Death

Consider all the pain of this life. The pain of sickness, weariness, despair, loneliness. The physical injuries, emotional wounds, spiritual evils, the tears of loss. Consider the vast wickedness of man in this life.

In paradise, every evil is banished. Every wickedness is gone. Every iniquity is no more.

> And death shall be no more, nor mourning, nor crying, nor sorrow, shall be any more, for the former things are passed away. And he that sat on the throne, said: Behold, I make all things new (Apoc. xxi. 4, 5).

There in our blessed homeland there is no uncertainty about God, for we shall see Him *face to face. Now I know in part; but then I shall know even as I am known* (I Cor. xiii. 12). There is no fear of judgment, *for we have passed over judgment* (Jn. v. 24). There is no anxiety of separation, for then truly *what shall separate us from the love of Christ?* (Rom. viii. 35).

As the baptismal rite foreshadows, "But you, evil spirit, depart, for the judgment of God has come." Heaven is the definitive judgment of God against all evil forever. Then will God put right what is wrong, straighten what is crooked, and revive what is dead. *And hell and death were cast into the pool of fire* (Apoc. xx. 14).

Then there will be the peace of Christ through the reign of Christ. The prophet Micheas saw it and rejoiced:

> And it shall come to pass in the last days, that the mountain of the house of the Lord shall be prepared in the top of mountains, and high above the hills: and people shall flow to it. And many nations shall come in haste, and say: Come, let us go up to the mountain of the Lord,

and to the house of the God of Jacob: and he will teach us of his ways, and we will walk in his paths ... and they shall beat their swords into ploughshares, and their spears into spades: nation shall not take sword against nation: neither shall they learn war any more. And every man shall sit under his vine, and under his fig tree, and there shall be none to make them afraid: for the mouth of the Lord of hosts hath spoken... we will walk in the name of the Lord our God for ever and ever (Mic. 4:1–5).

Image of Natural Beauty

Even after the fall of man, God has not left the natural world without the tranquility of beauty, which is a glimpse of the world to come. The saints have used this beauty to contemplate paradise. St. Francis de Sales:

Represent to yourself a lovely calm night, when the heavens are bright with innumerable stars: add to the beauty of such a night the utmost beauty of a glorious summer's day — the sun's brightness not hindering the clear shining of moon or stars, and then be sure that it all falls immeasurably short of the glory of Paradise. O bright and blessed country, O sweet and precious place![189]

Consider the sentiment you feel on beholding the great glory of the natural world's most awesome wonders. The vast reaches of the heavens and the stars, the endless stretch of the sea, the height of mountains and the expanse of the forests and meadows. Remember the sweet fragrance of spring, the song

---

[189] St. Francis de Sales, *Introduction to the Devout Life*, Ch. 16.

of birds, and the freshness of the morning air. Then know for certain these things are drops in the ocean of the glory of paradise. Even still, the natural world serves as a powerful icon of the world to come. In our finite existence, we find a great boon for meditation in the beauty and immensity of creation.

The Love of the Saints and
the Hope of Reunion with Lost Loved Ones

St. Francis de Sales tells us to meditate on the love of the saints:

> Imagine yourself alone with your good angel in an open plain, as was Tobit on his way to Rages. Suppose the Angel to set before you Paradise, full of delights and joys; and on the other hand Hell, with all its torments … your good Angel is urging you with all his might to [choose heaven], offering you countless graces on God's part, countless helps to attain to it[.]

> …Behold [Christ's] mother yearning over you with maternal tenderness — "Courage, my child, do not despise the Goodness of my Son, or my earnest prayers for thy salvation." Behold the Saints, who have left you their example, the millions of holy souls who long after you, desiring earnestly that you may one day be for ever joined to them in their song of praise, urging upon you that the road to Heaven is not so hard to find as the world would have you think. "Press on boldly, dear friend," — they cry. "Whoso will ponder well the path by which we came hither, will discover that we

attained to these present delights by sweeter joys than any this world can give."[190]

The great glory of the saints is the burning charity they hold toward the wayfaring soul — even us sinners. They have not ceased to yearn for your salvation since before you called upon them for aid. They still labor — if it can be called labor — for your eternal felicity and joy. At one with God, their only longing is to share this peace with more souls. Our Blessed Mother above all tenderly desires your union with all the saints in Christ. As the perfect mother, she burns with love for your soul.

Consider the sound of their chorus to which they invite you, rising infinitely in praising the mercy of God. The most beautiful and exquisite music you have ever heard is like foul noise in comparison. Once, St. Francis heard the sound of an angel playing an instrument, and he nearly died for joy.[191] Consider the beauty of the voice of the Virgin Mother above all the rest. De Sales says, "even as the newly-fledged nightingale learns to sing from the elder birds, so by our sacred communing with the Saints we shall learn better to pray and sing the praises of the Lord."[192]

Consider, too, the hope of finding in that heavenly country the loved ones we have lost. The children who were lost will run to you. Your parents will embrace you. If they have gained eternal life, then without a doubt they have longed for you and prayed for you as all the saints. Consider the love of all the saints, beckoning you to lift your heart to paradise and come.

The Love of God

But all these are what St. Alphonsus calls "the least of the blessings of paradise."[193] The true joy of paradise is the vision

---

[190] Ibid., ch. 17.
[191] St. Alphonsus, *op. cit.*
[192] St. Francis de Sales, *op. cit.*, Ch. 16.
[193] St. Alphonsus, *op. cit.*

of God the Blessed Trinity and glory of union with Him forever. Remember a time when you were filled with divine consolations. Remember those moments when God filled you with spiritual sweetness or joy in Him. Then know that these too are drops in the ocean.

Just as the immensity of the heavens far exceeds the greatest works of man, so too the consolation of God in paradise far exceeds every glimpse of His love on Earth. *According to the height of the heaven above the earth: he hath strengthened his mercy towards them that fear him* (Ps. cii. 11). When God touched your soul to show you His love, did you not rejoice in Him? So too you shall rejoice in Heaven in His great love for you, yet immeasurably more beyond all telling. The countless words, works, and labors of all the saints for two thousand years have not sufficed to begin to tell all His praises. And in Heaven, only eternity can provide enough space for His praise — and that only in our human capacity.

Consider your creation out of nothing. Before you existed, what did you do to deserve to be? It was the love of God that created you as an individual, unique soul. It was the love of God that provided you what was necessary for your growth and sustenance. The charity of God called you out of nothing and called you to life with Him.

Consider the Heart of Jesus Christ that became incarnate to seek your soul as the good shepherd seeks the lost sheep. Consider the Passion of Jesus, expiating your sins and washing you *white as snow* (Ps. l. 9). *Faint and weary, Thou hast sought me, on the Cross of suffering bought me.* It was for you that He shed His blood and breathed His last breath. It was for you that He rose again and showed you the glory of His wounds. *He delivered me because he desired me* (Ps. xvii. 20).

It was for this love that the saints joyfully received the torments of fire and the sword. It was for this love that the saints watched and fasted and prayed. It was for this love that they journeyed over land and sea and died to bring you the Faith and save your soul. Because *the sufferings of this life are not worthy to be compared to the glory to come* (Rom. viii. 18). Receive *Christ in you, the hope of glory* (Col. i. 27), and long for eternal life with all spiritual desire.

Summary Lists of
Our Forefathers' Daily Meditation & Practice

These lists are taken from the 1962 Roman Daily Missal
published by Angelus Press as well as the Saint Ambrose
Prayer Book published by Lancelot Andrews Press, 1st Ed.
V. Rev. Fr. J. Guy Winfrey, editor. The Duties of State in Life
are taken from Prümmer, nos. 461ff.

Duties of your state in Life

Duties of the supernatural order: give glory to God by
saving your soul; maintain your soul in a state of grace by
frequenting the Sacraments and fulfilling the six precepts of
the Church and the Ten Commandments; overcome sin and
grow in virtue; die in a state of grace.

Duties of the married:
Mutual duties: mutual love of affection and service; life in
common.
Husband duties: to love his wife as Christ did the Church;
provide for and protect his wife and children; to administer
family property wisely.
Wife duties: to submit to her husband; to properly care for
education of children and the home.
Children duties: show parents love, reverence, and obedience

Duties at the workplace:
Employer duties: treat employees with kindness; instruct and
correct employees; provide for religious observance; pay a
just wage to allow a man's wife to care for the children at
home.
Employee duties: due obedience and reverence; faithful
service by never stealing employer's time with personal
matters.

A Basic Rule of Life

1. To hear Mass on every Sunday and Holy Day of Obligation
2. To receive Holy Communion only after careful preparation including fasting, prayer and Confession if necessary
3. To make an examination of conscience every day and to go to Confession once a month. Choose one virtue each month to acquire. Repeat as much as necessary. Consider seriously at least every month your approaching death.
4. To say one third of the Holy Rosary (five decades) every day
5. To fast and abstain on every Friday of the year (excluding Solemnities)
6. To begin Lent with a definite written rule
7. To give alms to the needy and support my church
8. To practice Mental Prayer for 15 minutes each day, particularly on the Passion of our Lord.
9. To devote some time each week to reading the Holy Scriptures or learning about the faith
10. On hearing the Holy Name of Jesus profaned, to say at least in one's heart "Blessed be the Name of Jesus" as an act of reparation and intercession

The Ten Commandments

1. *I am the Lord thy God. Thou shalt not have strange Gods before Me.*
2. *Thou shalt not take the name of the Lord thy God in vain*
3. *Remember that thou keep holy the Sabbath day*
4. *Honor thy father and thy mother*
5. *Thou shalt not kill*
6. *Thou shalt not commit adultery*
7. *Thou shalt not steal*

8. *Thou shalt not bear false witness against thy neighbor*
9. *Thou shalt not covet thy neighbor's wife*
10. *Thou shalt not covet thy neighbor's house*

The Six Precepts of the Church

1. To hear Mass on Sundays and Holy Days of Obligation
2. To fast and abstain on the days commanded
3. To confess our sins at least once a year
4. To receive the Blessed Sacrament at Easter or within the time appointed
5. To contribute to the support of our Pastors
6. Not to solemnize marriage at the forbidden times; nor to marry persons within the forbidden degrees of kindreds, or otherwise prohibited by the Church, nor secretly

The Seven Sacraments

1. Baptism
2. Confirmation
3. Holy Eucharist
4. Confession (Reconciliation)
5. Extreme Unction (Anointing of the Sick)
6. Holy Orders
7. Matrimony

The Three Theological Virtues

1. Faith
2. Hope
3. Charity (Love)

The Four Cardinal Virtues

1. Prudence
2. Justice
3. Fortitude
4. Temperance

The Seven Gifts of the Holy Spirit

1. Wisdom
2. Understanding
3. Counsel
4. Fortitude
5. Knowledge
6. Piety
7. Fear of the Lord

The Twelve Fruits of the Holy Spirit

1. Charity
2. Joy
3. Peace
4. Patience
5. Longanimity
6. Goodness
7. Benignity
8. Mildness
9. Fidelity
10. Modesty
11. Continence
12. Chastity

The Seven Spiritual Works of Mercy

1. To give counsel to the doubtful
2. To instruct the ignorant
3. To admonish sinners
4. To comfort the afflicted
5. To forgive offenses
6. To bear patiently the troublesome
7. To pray for the living and the dead

The Seven Corporal Works of Mercy

1. To feed the hungry
2. To give drink to the thirsty
3. To clothe the naked
4. To shelter the needy
5. To visit the sick
6. To visit the imprisoned
7. To bury the dead

The Eight Beatitudes

1. Blessed are the poor in spirit; for theirs is the kingdom of heaven
2. Blessed are the meek; for they shall possess the land
3. Blessed are they that mourn; for they shall comforted
4. Blessed are they that hunger and thirst for justice; for they shall be filled
5. Blessed are the merciful; for they shall obtain mercy
6. Blessed are the clean of heart; for they shall see God
7. Blessed are the peacemakers; for they shall be called the children of God
8. Blessed are they that suffer persecution for justice' sake; for theirs is the kingdom of heaven

TIMOTHY S. FLANDERS

The Seven Last Words of Our Lord

1. Father, forgive them, for they know not what they do.
2. Amen, I say to thee, this day thou shalt be with Me in paradise.
3. Woman, Behold thy Son; behold, thy Mother.
4. My God, My God, why hast Thou forsaken Me?
5. I thirst.
6. It is finished.
7. Father, into Thy hands I commend my spirit.

The Seven Stages of Sin

1. Suggestion
2. Pleasure
3. Consent
4. Act
5. Habit
6. Slavery
7. Spiritual Blindness

Why One Should Sorrow for Sin

1. Because sin grieves and offends God
2. Because sin is yielding to the Evil One
3. Because sin brought the fall of man
4. Because sin brought sorrow and suffering
5. Because sin caused the Death of Christ
6. Because sin separates us from God
7. Because sin crucifies Jesus Christ afresh
8. Because sin resists the Holy Spirit
9. Because sin ruins our character
10. Because sin deadens our conscience
11. Because sin prevents the working of Grace
12. Because sin imperils our immortal souls
13. Because *the wages of sin is death*

WHEN THE GATES OF HELL PREVAIL

Why One Should Go to Confession

1. It shows sorrow for sin
2. It expresses the need for God's Grace
3. It strengthens the will and enlightens the mind
4. It increases the beauty of holiness
5. It brings peace to the mind and soul
6. It keeps from presumption and pride
7. It seeks pardon in God's appointed way
8. It releases from the eternal punishment
9. It reduces temporal punishment
10. It cleanses in the Blood of Jesus Christ
11. It restores to a state of Grace
12. It fits the soul for death and judgment
13. It show Faith, Hope, and Charity
14. It marks the Cross in our lives
15. It leaves nothing undone to ensure pardon

Three Marks of Real Penance

1. In the Heart – Contrition
2. In the Mouth – Confession
3. In the Life – Amendment

The Seven Penitential Psalms

1. Ps. 6 *Lord, not in anger*
2. Ps. 31 (32) *Blessed are those*
3. Ps. 37 (38) *Lord, not in anger*
4. Ps. 50 (51) *Have mercy on me, O God*
5. Ps. 101 (102) *O Lord, hear*
6. Ps. 129 (130) *Out of the depths*
7. Ps. 142 (143) *O Lord, hear*

The Seven Deadly Sins and Contrary Virtues

1. Pride..................Humility
2. Covetousness.....Liberality
3. Lust....................Chastity
4. Wrath................Meekness
5. Gluttony.............Temperance
6. Envy...................Brotherly love
7. Sloth..................Diligence

Ways of Conquering the Seven Deadly Sins

In General: Prayer, fasting and alms; practice of self-denial, detachment and recollection in God's presence.

Pride: Cultivation of simplicity; seeking meekness and humility of heart; meditations upon the life of Our Lord

Anger: Practicing self-control; silence before speaking; signing the Cross; recognizing the possibly of acts of violence; praying for others or self; rendering good for evil; kindness, patience, forbearance, forgiveness.

Envy: Cultivating charity, magnanimity, rejoicing in the joy or success of others.

Covetousness: Caring little for earthy things; never hoarding; being generous to man grateful to God, giving liberally to the Church and all good works; sharing with others.

Gluttony: Ruling our desires; being temperate and moderate; fasting; avoiding excess; taking less than desired.

Lust: Cultivating purity in thought, word, and deed; refusing to look at, speak or think of suggestive things; avoiding sources of temptation including movies, music or the internet; regular habits; exercise; prayer; fasting; flight in special bodily temptations; recognizing the awful consequences of lust.

Sloth: Living by Rule; being with useful or profitable employment; doing our duties conscientiously to the best of our ability as in the sight of God, for God's glory; taking proper rest or recreation, but resisting idleness or laziness; singing spiritual hymns or psalms while we work.

Sins Against the Holy Spirit

1. Presumption upon God's mercy
2. Despair
3. Impugning the known truth
4. Envy of another's spiritual good
5. Obstinacy in sin
6. Final Impenitence

Sins Crying to Heaven for Vengeance

1. Willful murder
2. The sin of Sodom
3. Oppression of the poor
4. Defrauding laborers of their wages

Nine Ways of Being Accessory to Another's Sin

1. By counsel
2. By command
3. By consent
4. By provocation
5. By praise or flattery
6. By concealment
7. By partaking
8. By silence
9. By defense of the ill done

Three Eminently Good Works

1. Prayer
2. Fasting
3. Alms (or works of mercy)

Three Evangelical Counsels

1. Poverty
2. Chastity
3. Obedience

The Four Last Things

1. Death
2. Judgment
3. Heaven
4. Hell

Subjects for Daily Meditation

Remember, O Christian Soul, that thou hast this day and every day of thy life:

God to glorify
Jesus to imitate
The angels and saints to invoke
A soul to save
A body to mortify
Sins to expiate
Virtues to acquire
Hell to avoid
Heaven to gain
Eternity to prepare for
Time to profit by
Neighbors to edify
The world to despise
Devils to combat
Passions to subdue
Death perhaps to suffer
And judgment to undergo

Essential Books for Every Family's Library

Prayer Books

- *A Manual of Prayers: For the Use of the Catholic Laity* (Prepared and Published by Order of the Third Plenary Council of Baltimore)
- *The Raccolta*
- *Blessed Be God Prayer Book*

Spiritual Classics

- *The Institutes* by St. John Cassian
- *The Conferences* by St. John Cassian
- *The Ladder of Divine Ascent* by St. John Climacus
- *Imitation of Christ* by Thomas à Kempis
- *Introduction to the Devout* Life by St. Francis de Sales
- *The Spiritual Combat* by Dom Scupoli
- *The Secret of the Rosary* by St. Louis de Montfort
- *True Devotion to Mary* by St. Louis de Montfort

Catechism

- The Roman Catechism
- The Baltimore Catechism
- The Catechism of Pius X
- *The Catechism of the Catholic Church*
- *Credo: a Compendium of the Catholic Faith* by Bishop Athanasius Schneider

Doctrine

- Enchiridion Symbolorum ("Denzinger")[194]
- Fundamentals of Catholic Dogma[195]

Moral Theology

- Prümmer[196]
- *Made by God, Made for God: Catholic Morality Explained* by Matthew Minerd

---

[194] Current edition: Heinrich Denzinger, *Enchiridion Symbolorum* (Ignatius Press, 2013).
[195] Current edition: Ludwig Ott, *Fundamentals of Catholic Dogma* (Baronius: 2005).
[196] Current edition: Dominic Prümmer, *Handbook of Moral Theology* (Benedictus Books, 2022).

Bibliography

"Facebook founder warns of social media addiction." *Good Morning America.* Nov 10, 2017. <https://www.youtube.com/watch?v=LPwR1i-sWpo>, accessed October 24, 2023.

À Kempis, Thomas. *The Imitation of Christ.*

Anonymous, *The Life of Saint John Vianney, The Cure of Ars.* Joseph Schaefer: New York, 1911.

Aquinas, Thomas. *The Summa.*

Augustine. *City of God.*

___. *Commentary on the Psalms.*

___. *Tractates on the Gospel of John.* CUA Press: 1994.

Aumann, Jordan. *Spiritual Theology.* Sheed and Ward: 1980.

Benedict. *Rule.*

Bowles, Nellie. "A Dark Consensus About Screens and Kids Begins to Emerge in Silicon Valley: 'I am convinced the devil lives in our phones.'" *New York Times.* Oct. 26, 2018.

Cahill, E. *The Framework of a Christian State.* Roman Catholic Books reprint 1932.

Da Bergamo, Cajetan. *Humility of Heart.* Translated by Herbert Vaughan. TAN reprint, 2018.

De Groot, J. V. *Summa Apologeticade Ecclesia Catholica.* Ratisbonae, 1906.

De Mattei, Roberto. "Who Was the Worst Pope in the History of the Church?" *Corrispondenza Romana* (December 4th, 2019). Translated by Francesca Romana. <https://rorate-caeli.blogspot.com/2019/12/de-mattei-who-was-worst-pope-in-history.html>, accessed March 16, 2021.

de Montfort, Louis. *True Devotion to Mary.*

de Sales, Francis. *Introduction to the Devout Life.*

Didache, The.

Dostoevsky, Fyodor. *The Brothers Karamazov.* Translated by Constance
Garnett. New York: the Lowell Press, 1912.

Enchiridion Indulgentiarum Normae et Concessiones. Third Printing.
Libreria Editrice Vaticana: 2006. USCCB, 2013.

Fahlbusch, Erwin and Geoffrey Bromiley, editors. *The Encyclopedia of
Christianity.* Eerdmans: 2005.

Flanders, T. S. "On the Limits of Papal Infallibility," *OnePeterFive.* June
29, 2022. <https://onepeterfive.com/limits-papal-infallibility/>,
accessed November 13, 2023.

___. *Introduction to the Holy Bible for Traditional Catholics.* Our Lady
of Victory Press: 2019.

___. *City of God vs. City of Man.* Our Lady of Victory Press, 2021.

Garrigou-Lagrange, Fr. Reginald. *The Three Ages of the Spiritual Life.*
Herder: 1947. 2 Volumes.

Gibbons, James Cardinal. *Faith of our Fathers.* 110th edition. New York:
P. J. Kennedy & Sons, 1917.

Guéranger, Prosper. *The Liturgical Year.*

Hardon, John. "The Influence of Marxism in the United
States." *Mindszenty Report.* Cardinal Mindszenty Foundation,
August 1998.

Hahn, Scott and Curtis Mitch, eds. *The Ignatius Catholic Study Bible:
New Testament.* San Francisco, CA: Ignatius, 2010.

Ignatius of the Side of Jesus. *The School of Jesus Crucified.* 1866.

John Cassian, *Conferences.*

John Chrysostom. *Homily II on Acts.*

Joyce, G. "The Church." *The Catholic Encyclopedia.* New York: Robert
Appleton Company, 1908.

Kwasniewski, Peter. "Lessons from Church History: A Brief Review of Papal Lapses." *OnePeterFive.* Aug 6, 2018. <https://onepeterfive.com/lessons-church-history-papal-lapses/>, accessed October 23, 2023.

La Salette Missionaries. "The Message of La Salette." <https://www.lasalette.org/about-la-salette/apparition/the-story/705-the-message-of-la-salette.html>, accessed November 13, 2023.

Leo XIII. *Divinum Illud Munus.* 1897.

Liguori, Alphonsus. *Means to Acquire the Love of God.*

___. *Moral Theology.* Translated by Ryan Grant. Mediatrix Press,

___. *Preparation for Death.*

___. *Sermons for the Sundays of the Year.* 8th edition. Translated by Nicholas Callan. Dublin: Duffy & Sons, 1882.

Maritain, Jacques. *Peasant of the Garonne.* Translated by Michael Cuddihy. New York: Holy, 1966.

Meyendorff, John. *The Primacy of Peter.* Crestwood, NY: St. Vladimir's Seminary Press, 1992.

Newman, John Henry. "Discourse 17: The Glories of Mary for the Sake of Her Son." *Newman Reader.* National Institute for Newman Studies, 2007. <http://newmanreader.org/works/discourses/discourse17.html>. Accessed March 25, 2021.

Ott, Ludwig. *Fundamentals of Catholic Dogma.* Baronius Press, 2018.

Pègues, R. P. Thomas. *Catechism of the Summa.* 1922.

Paul VI. *Discourse to the Roman Nobility.* January 14, 1964.

Pius X. *Catechism of Pius X.*

Pius XI. *Divini Redemptoris.* 1937.

___. *Quas Primas.* 1925.

___. *Quadragesimo Anno.* 1931.

___. *Rite Expiatis.* 1926.

Prümmer, Dominic. "The Catholic Teaching of Conscience," *OnePeterFive* (Jan 27, 2022) <https://onepeterfive.com/the-catholic-teaching-on-conscience>, accessed November 5, 2023.

___. *Handbook of Moral Theology.* Centenary Edition. *Benedictus Books,* 2022.

Rex, Richard. *Henry VIII and the English Reformation.* Macmillan International Higher Education: 2006.

Ripperger, Chad. "Virtues and Vices." *Sensus Traditionis.* 2016. <https://sensustraditionis.org/Virtues.pdf>, accessed October 25, 2023.

___. *Magisterial Authority.* Sensus Traditionis Press, 2014.

___. *The Binding Force of Tradition.* Sensus Traditionis, 2013.

___. *Topics on Tradition.* Sensus Traditionis Press, 2013.

Roman Catechism, The.

Salaverri, Joachim and Michaele Nicolau. *Sacrae Theologiae Summa.* Translated by Kenneth Baker. 3rd edition. Keep the Faith, 2015. Original printing 1956.

Schneider, Athanasius. *Credo: Compendium of the Catholic Faith.* Sophia, 2023.

Schneider, Floyd. *Mark Challenges the Aeneid.* Wipf & Stock Publishers, 2019.

Scupoli, Dom Lorenzo. *Of Interior Peace or the Path to Paradise. The Spiritual Combat.* Scriptoria Books: 2012.

Shaw, Joseph. *The Liturgy, the Family, and the Crisis of Modernity: Essays of a Traditional Catholic.* Os Justi Press, 2023.

Solovyov, Vladimir. *Russia and the Universal Church.* Translated by Herbert Rees. London: Centenary Press, 1948.

Spirago, Francis. *The Catechism Explained.* 1899.

Ybarra, E. "Pope Victor I (189-98) & the Roman Primacy – Critical Analysis." Jan. 13, 2017.

<https://erickybarra.wordpress.com/2017/01/13/pope-victor-i-189-98-the-roman-primacy-critical-analysis/>, accessed October 23, 2023.

____. *The Papacy*. Emmaus Road, 2023.

Chapters 3, 5, 6, 12, 13, 14, 15, 16, 17, 18, 21, 23, 25 originally published at *OnePeterFive.*

Chapters 2, 4, 9, 10, 22, 24 originally published in *Catholic Family News*

Other chapters originally appeared at Meaningofcatholic.com or have not been previously published.

Made in the USA
Middletown, DE
09 September 2024

60635128R00149